THE FOREST

Walter Kümmerly

THE FOREST

Translated from
the German
by Ewald Osers

Robert B. Luce Co., Inc.

Washington – New York

Copyright © 1973 by Kümmerly & Frey, Geographical Publishers, Berne/Switzerland
Published in the United States 1973
All rights reserved, including the right to reproduce this book, or
parts thereof, in any form except for the inclusion of brief quotations in a review.
Library of Congress Card Catalog Number 73-9056

Cartography, photolithography and color printing:
Kümmerly & Frey, Graphical Institute, Berne/Switzerland
Clichés: Ernst Kreienbühl & Cie, Lucerne
Composition, printing and binding: Stämpfli + Cie AG, Berne
Printed in Switzerland   ISBN 0-88331-059-7

Dust jacket: Illecillewaet Valley with Mount Sir Donald in British Columbia
Color photograph by Nicholas Morant, Banff, Alberta (Canada)

Photographs

Almasy, Neuilly-sur-Seine (France)
Bavaria, München
Bechtel Helmut, Düsseldorf
Beringer & Pampaluchi, Zürich
Berney Henri-Maurice, Montreux
von Bonin Volker, Helsinki
Bosshard Hans, Zürich
Botanisches Institut der Universität Bern
Canadian Government Travel Bureau, Ottawa
Canadian National Film Board, Ottawa
Coleman Bruce, Hillingdon/Middlesex (England)
Danesch Othmar, Niedergösgen (Switzerland)
Eidgenössische Vermessungsdirektion, Bern
E. T. H. Zürich, Institut für Allgemeine Botanik
von Fellenberg G., Bern
Forest Research Station, Farnham (England)
Forest Service, U. S. Department of Agriculture, Washington D. C.
Forstwirtschaftliche Zentralstelle der Schweiz, Solothurn
Fotogram, Paris
Fronval, Champigny-sur-Marne (France)
Gardi René, Bern
Gohl Heinrich, Basel
Guggisberg C. A. W., Nairobi (Kenya)
Hagen Toni, U. N., New York
von Hirmer H., München
Hoa-Qui, Paris
Imber Walter, Laufen (Switzerland)
Koch Paolo, Zürich

Krüger Christoph, Wien
Kündig-Steiner Werner, Zürich
Lauber Konrad, Bern
Magnum Photos, Zürich:
    Bischoff Werner, Buri René,
    Lorrain Sergio, Cartier-Bresson Henri, Sochurek H.
Merckx Paul, Brussels
Mounicq, Paris
National Geographic Society, Washington D. C.
Nawrath Alfred, Bremen
News Agency Tass, Moscow
Office National du Tourisme Canadien, Paris
Tierbilder Okapia GmbH, Frankfurt am Main
Omnia, Keusen Hans, Bern
PIP Photos, New York
Press Agency Novosti, Moscow
Rau Werner, Stuttgart
Rausser Hans, Bern
Roebild, Frankfurt am Main
Schmid Oskar, Amriswil (Switzerland)
Trémellat, Marseille
U. S. National Park Service, Washington D. C.
Weidmann Karl, Los Teques (Venezuela)
Widmer Rudolf, Zofingen (Switzerland)
Winkelmann H. G., Solothurn (Switzerland)
Wolgensinger Photo Film, Zürich
World Wildlife Fund, Morges (Switzerland)

Contents

Man—
I keep you warm in freezing winter nights
I am your shade from scorching summer sun
The roof-joists of your house, your table's board
I am the bed in which you sleep at night
The wood of which your mighty ships are built
I am your pickaxe shaft, your cabin's door
The wood of both your cradle and your coffin
I am the bread of goodness, flower of beauty
Answer my prayer: Do not destroy me...

The World's Forests

Heinrich Lamprecht

The original home of the trees is in the forest–the most perfect piece of creation in the plant kingdom. Trees make up the forest, trees determine its form and its appearance. It is in the forest that we must observe the trees and listen to them if we want to understand them.

Which trees associate to form forests, what they look like and how they behave, how this forest or that is composed–all this depends primarily on prevailing climatic and soil conditions, unless Man by his encroachment has disfigured or destroyed the natural forest environment. Certainly the appearance of forests has been and is still being transformed over vast regions of the globe, but all too often they are devastated by crop and stock farming, timber felling and fire.

Forests nowadays cover roughly 15 million square miles or 34 per cent of the land area of the world. Of this total Europe and Africa account for 3.6 million, North and South America for just under 6 million, Russia, Asia and Australia for 5.2 million square miles. Twenty-five per cent of the land area of the earth is cultivated while 41 per cent has to be regarded as unproductive desert. Seventy per cent of the world's forests are State-owned; only 20 per cent belong to private individuals and 10 per cent to municipalities and other collective bodies.

The timber reserves in the commercially managed forests of the world are estimated at a total of 4,340,000 million cubic feet. The greatest supplies are owned by the U.S.S.R. with 2,100,000 million cubic feet; next follow North America with 850,000 million and Asia less the U.S.S.R. with 140,000 million cubic feet. Europe, though much smaller in area, nevertheless has a growing stock of nearly 350,000 million cubic feet, thanks to over 100 years' intensive forestry management. One aspect of this intensive management is the fact that felling per acre of forest is highest in Europe. It averages 33 cubic feet per acre per annum, compared with 8.6 in North America and 7 or less in the rest of the world.

Boreal coniferous forest belt and tropical forests

About 80 per cent of the world's total forested area is situated in two vast and originally compact zones of dense growth–in the north of the northern hemisphere and in the tropics.

The boreal coniferous forest belt extends from Alaska to Labrador, and from Scandinavia through Karelia and Siberia all the way to Kamchatka. Only a small number of species, such as spruce, pine, Siberian larch, fir and Arolla pine, make up these vast and magnificently uniform forests of the north. The only representatives of the otherwise varied realm of broadleaved trees are frost-resisting sturdy birches, willows and aspens. For their admirable strength in standing up to gales and snow, winter and frost, the trees of the lonely northern wastes are comparable to those of European high-alpine forests. And indeed they are very largely the same or closely related species: Siberian larch, Siberian fir and Siberian Arolla pine frequently take the place of their European relations, just as boreal and alpine coniferous forests have many other features in common. However, the mountain forest lacks that boundless horizon, the infinite wide open space which is the domain of the northern forest.

Totally different ecological conditions are encountered in the tropical forest belt which girdles the globe like a green band roughly between the tropics of Cancer and Capricorn. In contrast to the North, the tropics are the unchallenged realm of the broadleaved trees. In our own latitudes nature has not created anything even approaching the magnitude and splendor of the tropical forests. According to conservative estimates, tropical forests cover nearly 6 million square miles or roughly 40 per cent of the earth's total forest area. To this day large parts of this huge tropical forest zone are genuine no-man's land –inadequately explored or not explored at all. This is surprising as tropical forests with their vast quantities of timbers of all kinds represent a raw material reserve of high proportions, a reserve whose sensible utilization would be in the interest not only of the natives but of mankind generally.

Before turning to the tropical forest, that great unknown, let us cast a quick glance at the wide zone situated between boreal coniferous and tropical broadleaved forest, a zone embracing the whole of southern and Central Europe as well as large parts of North America and Asia. In these climatically temperate regions, favoring human settlement, the forest has been forced back further and further by man over hundreds and perhaps thousands of years. It has survived only on poor soil or on soil otherwise unsuitable for agriculture, and often also–though unfortunately not in all places where this would be necessary in the form of forest reservations. Only about 20 per cent of the total forest area is situated between boreal coniferous and tropical forest on the northern hemisphere and between tropical forest and the Antarctic on the southern hemisphere. The southern hemisphere, for climatic reasons, totally lacks a coniferous forest belt corresponding to the boreal one.

The Mediterranean area once harbored hard-leaf forests, made up of short-stemmed gnarled trees with thick bark and dull, hard, leathery foliage. These included various evergreen oaks and other species. Nowadays the olive is the characteristic tree of the Mediterranean countries. The original forests have nearly everywhere been destroyed by ruthless exploitation, fire, or goat grazing. Their place has been taken by low almost impenetrable scrub, the *maquis* or *macchia*. In California, where the degenerated hard-leaf forest likewise occupies large areas, it is known by the Spanish word *chaparral*. Frequently, however, the destructive process has gone much further and resulted in the total erosion by water or wind of the fertile top-soil. Vast karstified, sandy waste lands, real man-made deserts, throughout the hard-leaf zone testify to Man's short-sightedness. With an alarming poignancy they confirm the old saying that civilization and culture began with the felling of the first big tree in the primeval forest and will end when the axe is laid on the last one.

The plains and lower mountain levels of central Europe were originally covered by deciduous broadleaved forests whose place was taken in the higher mountains by coniferous forests. Our broadleaved trees such as beech, oak, maple, ash, elm, lime, cherry, birch and alder can be identified by tall slender stems, a richly ramified crown, bright delicate foliage, fresh green in spring, growth in summer, colorful turning of leaves in the fall, and shedding of the leaves and dormancy in winter. The yearly temperature pattern determines their entire existence and behavior. Among the conifers only the larch participates in this annual death and rebirth, while Norway spruce, white fir, pine and yew remain evergreen.

Deciduous forests, similar to those of Central Europe, are found in the temperate zones of North America and in East Asia. But the first glance reveals that American and Asian broadleaved and coniferous forests are richer in species than the corresponding European ones. To understand this striking difference under almost similar environmental conditions, we have to turn back the pages of our planet's history. There were trees growing and forests covering the earth as long ago as some 300 million years. The first tree-type plants came from the genera of Lycopodia and horsetails, whose descendants survive to this day as modest small low-height plants. Very early the first fern-type trees appeared. But these proto-trees and proto-forests flourished many millions of years before the arrival of the first man. Their remains have been preserved for us in our coal seams and are valuable sources of energy.

One geological period succeeded another, mountains were piled up and worn away, continents were flooded by oceans and once more released, plants died out and new ones took their place. Only the fossils preserved here and there testify to the great upheavals in which trees and forests participated and to which they were subject. Entire genera of trees and the forests in which they were dominant vanished for ever, re-emerged from other species, were forced back or destroyed, and always again reconquered the dry land. The conifers developed over the past 260 million years while the broadleaved trees set out on their victorious conquest some 130 million years ago.

In the Tertiary era about one million years ago—and we are now approaching the most recent geological past—there was a fairly uniform warm climate through the entire northern hemisphere. A somewhat similar and very varied flora covered the temperate zones of Asia, North America and Europe. Then, about 800,000 years ago, for reasons still largely unknown, the climate began to get colder. Temperatures dropped and glaciers advanced from the mountains to cover the plains. Faced with their icy breath, the vegetation retreated. In central Europe this retreat encountered the often insuperable obstacle of mountain ranges running predominantly from east to west. A large number of plants, including many species of trees, were not successful in escaping. They fell victim to the cold. Only remnants of the original flora survived in the European zone and, following the last retreat of the glaciers some 10,000 years ago, were able to return to their former habitat insofar as such a reconquest was not ruled out by the climate which continued to remain cooler even after the Ice Age. Thus the present-day flora of central Europe is only a poor and very incomplete copy of its original profusion.

Conditions were much more favorable on the North American continent because there the mountain ranges, generally running from north to south, did not impede the flight to warmer zones or only did so very slightly. North America's flora, in consequence, was decimated far less by the glaciers than that of Europe. East Asia very largely escaped the Ice Age and its murderous effects and therefore now possesses the most varied deciduous broadleaved forests. The history of our most recent geological past also explains why many an American or Asian tree thrives so well in our latitudes. After all, quite a few of them were native to Europe before the Ice Age. Many such strangers have been reintroduced by Man and now adorn our parks and gardens as valuable ornamental and decorative trees, as for instance the mighty sequoias, the ancient Gingko (or maidenhair tree) whose history spans the unimaginable period of roughly 200 million years, the tulip tree with its strangely lobed leaves and beautiful flowers, several large-flowering species of magnolia, the Ailanthus tree, various maples with their magnificent autumn tints, cherries from Asia, and others. Only a few of them have become domiciled as forest trees, such as the locust or pseudo-acacia, the Douglas fir, the Weymouth pine and the red oak.

The southern hemisphere also lacks the deciduous broadleaved forest. The southern continents only rarely extend into the temperate latitude and then only as relatively narrow land tongues (like southern South America). Their climate is therefore governed by the oceans while in the northern hemisphere the climate is vitally affected by the much larger land masses.

On the other hand, both north and south of the tropical belt, in the mild humid temperate climate of the ocean-affected coastal areas and islands we find flourishing temperate rain forests and, where summer precipitation is slightly less, the laurel forests. This applies to Pacific North America, to southern Chile, to New Zealand and Tasmania, to central China and to the Canary Islands. These forests, too, have already suffered large-scale devastation by Man. Nevertheless, the surviving forests are impressive testimony to their original beauty and outstanding vitality.

Extensive temperate rain forests exist nowadays also in the "little South" of Chile, a landscape where water and forest, mountains and trees combine to produce a uniquely beautiful and enchanting harmony. In the clear water of lonely lakes are reflected the perfect pyramids of extinct or still active volcanoes,

the white caps of the Andean ranges, the dark foliage of tall slender southern beeches, the species *Notho-fagus*. With their smooth grey stems and umbrella-shaped crowns they are indeed strongly reminiscent of the familiar European and North American beeches. But they are mostly evergreen and the forests they form are unlike our spacious canopied beech forests; they are much more luxuriant and richer. Their luxuriance, enhanced by frequent occurrence of lianas, tree ferns and epiphytes, almost resembles the cloud forests of the high tropical mountain ranges.

Forests between the two tropics

Genuine tropical forests are found only between the two tropics in America, Africa and south-east Asia as far as Australia. Their great variety and their wealth of trees and plants cannot be visualized by any-one who has not visited them. To quote just one figure: in the Amazon forest alone more than 3,000 dif-ferent species of trees have so far been studied in detail or at least recorded.

If we steer a ship towards a flat tropical coast or, better still, into a harbour situated in the estuary of a big river, we encounter the tropical forest even before we step out on dry land. Our first welcome is from the mangrove swamp forest, the forest which grows in the sea.

The preferred habitat of mangroves is in the tidal zones which are virtually dry at low water but are totally flooded by salt or brackish water at high tide. Trees thriving in the sea must possess quite special proper-ties to withstand their extremely difficult environmental conditions. Most species are incapable of doing so. The mangroves, on the other hand, about half a dozen or a dozen species, are evidently able to do so– in fact, they grow to a height of 65 feet or more. They have developed a great variety of highly effective means for solving the many problems which their unusual location poses for them. To quote but a few ex-amples: normally a tree on muddy soil, which is completely flooded for a period each day and very badly aerated, would suffocate from lack of oxygen. The mangrove counters this mortal danger by developing aerial roots as respiratory organs. In some species these spring from the stem, often right up in the crown and hang down like ropes: this applies mainly to *Rhizophora mangle*. Others grow from the ground roots and, according to the depth of flooding, project more or less from the water. They form extensive com-pact fields of breathing pegs, as in the case of *Avicennia nitida*. Others yet stand on stilt roots or ensure their oxygen supply by developing knee roots which, twisted like serpents, emerge from the mud and dive below the surface in a tight loop a short way off.

Even more remarkable is the manner in which the mangroves ensure their propagation. At high tide their seeds would drop straight into the water, and those falling on the ground at low tide would be washed away at the next flooding. Only very occasionally would a seed achieve germination and the young seedling mature. Such occasional lucky chances, however, would not be enough to ensure the future of the mangrove forest. Once a plant which has accidentally reached a site and established itself there is no longer able, for whatever reason, to propagate in sufficient numbers, its species, after the death of the individual, will have certainly lost its struggle for that particular site. The situation of the mangroves would seem hopeless but in fact is not. They have overcome this particular difficulty. Their ripe seeds do not, as is usual, drop to the ground but remain suspended and germinate on the parent tree. The mangrove species, exceptionally among trees, are viviparous. Not seeds but more or less fully developed young seedlings drop from the trees. If they fall on the ground they instantly strike root. But even if they are swept away by the next high tide or if they drop into the water from the start everything is not lost. Mangrove seedlings are excellent floaters. Careful investigations have shown that *Rhizophora* plants can survive floating in the sea for three months and sometimes even longer. If during that time they are washed ashore they strike root at once and are presumably safe. In spite of nature's solicitous provision a large part, indeed by far the greatest part, of the young plants die. They are drowned in the sea, parched on the scorching sands, battered by the waves. Yet the annual production of young seedlings is so great that the exceedingly small number of survivors is more than adequate to replace the old trees which die.

As a matter of fact, the mangroves not only stand their ground but in shallow water they are even capable of steadily conquering new territories. Their densely interwoven and matted above-ground roots act as a breakwater and trap mud and sand, leaves, twigs and all forest waste and thus create soil. Pioneers in the word's truest sense, they advance into the water. Admittedly, their gains at the front are offset by losses in the hinterland. As soon as this is sufficiently far away from the sea and the soil has been sufficiently built up to be outside the tidal range other tree species, now capable of competition under the greatly improved environmental conditions, oust the mangroves. More demanding and richer forest communities take their place.

Rain forests in the tropical lowlands and mountains

The equatorial rain forest, the most perfect and most magnificent embodiment of the ecological associa-tion we call forest, grows and luxuriates in the hot humid lowlands. To develop its massive scale and richness it requires a constant high level of heat throughout the year–an average annual temperature of about 68 to 82°F (20 to 28°C)–and a precipitation of at least 70 inches (1,800 mm) spread evenly over the whole year. The largest rain forest zone is in South America, centered on the Amazon and Orinoco river systems. A second center embraces the Congo, the Cameroons and the Guinea coast. The Asian lowland rain forests extend from western India through Ceylon, Burma and Thailand to Indo-China, in-cluding the Philippine and Indonesian archipelagos. One's first impression when faced with the vegeta-tive wealth, with the abundant vitality of such a forest, is one of confusion. The canopies of the tree-tops form three or four interlinked storeys, one above the other. Frequently the lower ones block the view of the upper storeys, and only rarely does the sky shimmer through a small opening in the many-layered canopy or a sunray penetrate the green twilight. Ahead, behind and to both sides the eye meets a green wall of trees, small trees, tall and low bushes, and herbaceous plants. This extraordinary plenitude of plant life and the unique luxuriance of its development in the lowland rain forest is due to the uniform hothouse climate throughout the year, a climate which has a generally enervating effect on Man. Well over 10,000 tree species, not to mention other plants, are known at present and have been described, but new ones are still being discovered to extend an already long list. On an area of a single hectare (about 2.5 acres) sixty to over 100 different tree species are found together. It is their colorful mixture that pro-duces the characteristic picture of the rain forest. The topmost open canopy is formed by giants growing singly or in groups to a height of 165 to 200 feet and more, and having a diameter of over 6 feet. Below their gigantic crowns, which are often entirely overgrown with lianas, lies a second compact storey of trees 100 to 130 feet tall. Lower down lie a third and a fourth storey as well as a usually rather sparse layer of bushes which, in the green shade inside the forest, suffers from a shortage of light.

Gradually one finds one's bearings. Already one tree or another may be distinguished from its neighbor by some special characteristic. The rain forest offers such superb ecological conditions that nature's lux-ury-loving creatures thrive here, species which would have long died in the harsher conditions of less fa-vored regions. Perhaps the first to be noticed are the slender silvery grey palm trees which, according to the species they belong to, spread their giant fronds in the topmost canopies or in the understorey. Some palm species have even turned into creepers. An example is the rotang palm or rattan,which can grow to a length of 1,000 feet. Its pinnate leaves terminate in tendrils many feet long and closely set with steel-hard hooklike spines. With these tendrils which are set in motion by every breath of air, the rattan searches its neighborhood for support, and once it gets its hooks anchored pulls itself up towards the life-giving light. Not only for this palm but also for many other light-seeking species which by their own strength are unable to grow up into the highest canopy the creeper form offers a convenient way of attaining a place in the sun with someone else's help. The liana cables and ropes, which can attain the thickness of an arm or more, therefore belong to the typical picture of the rain forest. Another strange feature is the gigantic plank buttresses around the bases of many trees, often starting at a height of 10 to 13 feet and, running obliquely downwards, reaching the ground several yards away from the stem proper. These narrow-backed triangular "fins", often arranged in a star shape, and the recesses formed between them lend the trees strength and elegance.

One of the most impressive features of the rain forest is the ability of many tree species to produce flowers from the stem. While it is often quite impossible to get a proper view of the magnificent blossoms up in the tree top, the stem flowers stand right before the eye of the observer. Quite apart from the fact that flowers bursting from the bark are something unusual, they frequently also are of quite extraordinary beauty as, for instance, the rose-like blossoms of various *Brownea* species which grow to over 6 inches and whose brilliant red contrasts magnificently with the tree's dark bark when struck by a shaft of sunlight penetrating the semi-darkness. Small wonder the native hunters and rangers call them forest roses. Strange and exotic also are the stemflowers of various species of the family of Lecytidaceae. Rust-coloured and yellow, hand-sized and flat, they are not remotely comparable in structure or appearance to any native European flower. At blossom time they cover the black-brown bark in their hundreds. Strange also are the fruits they produce. The size of a man's head, spherical and smooth, they hang by the dozen on the stems of certain species. It is to them that the tree owes its English name: cannonball tree. The cocoa tree, really more like a shrub, whose original home is the American tropical forest where it grows wild to this day, also produces flowers from its stem.

Even to list the commercially useful trees native to the rain forest of the lowlands would exceed the scope of this account. We must confine ourselves to a few brief hints. The milky sap of the Pará rubber tree, *Hevea brasiliensis,* was the source of the fabulous wealth created in the second half of the past century for Amazonia and, in particular, for Manaus, the center of the rubber trade. In this jungle town on the Rio Negro an opera house was built of imported Carrara marble and the most famous singers and actors gave guest performances there. To safeguard her rubber monopoly Brazil banned the export of the precious *Hevea* seeds. But in spite of the threat of heavy penalties they got to Asia by adventurous

World Map of Forest Zones

Scale 1:83,000,000

1	Tropical lowland rain forests, montane rain forests, cloud forests
2	Tropical rain-green forests, savanna, monsoon and dry forests
3	Subtropical forests, temperate-latitude forests, hard-leaf forests
4	Northern-climate coniferous forests of Asia, Europe and America
5	Woodless zones: deserts and icy wastes, cold steppes, cultivated areas

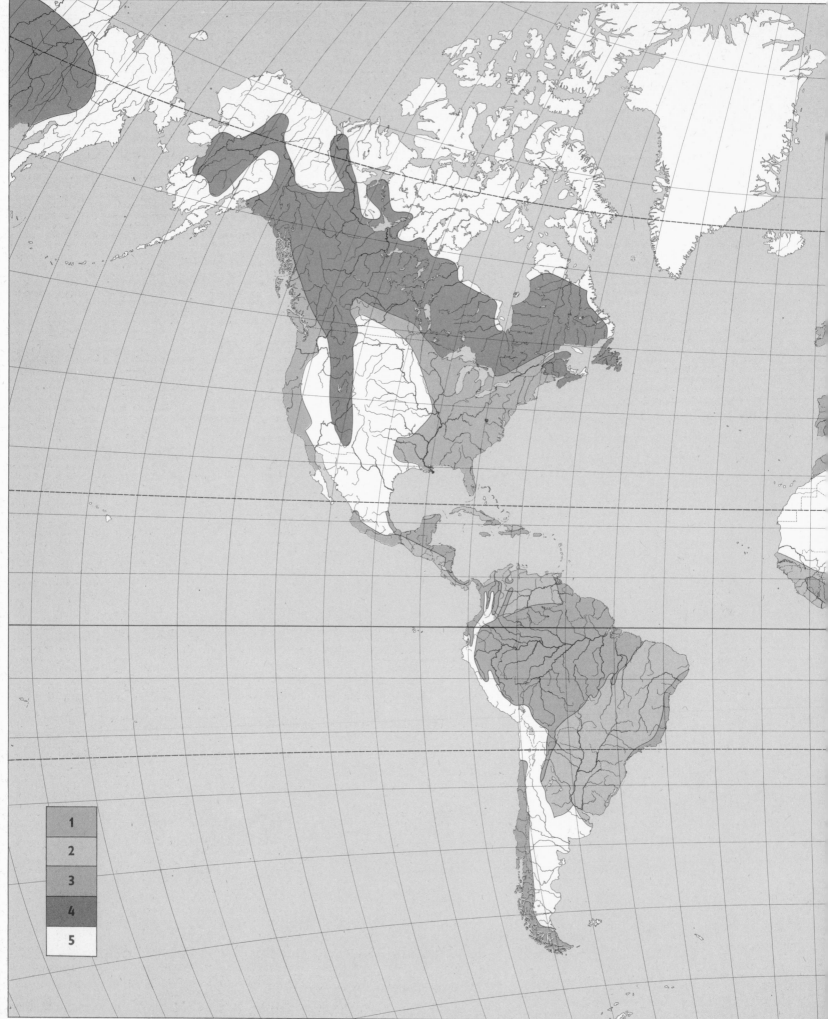

1
2
3
4
5

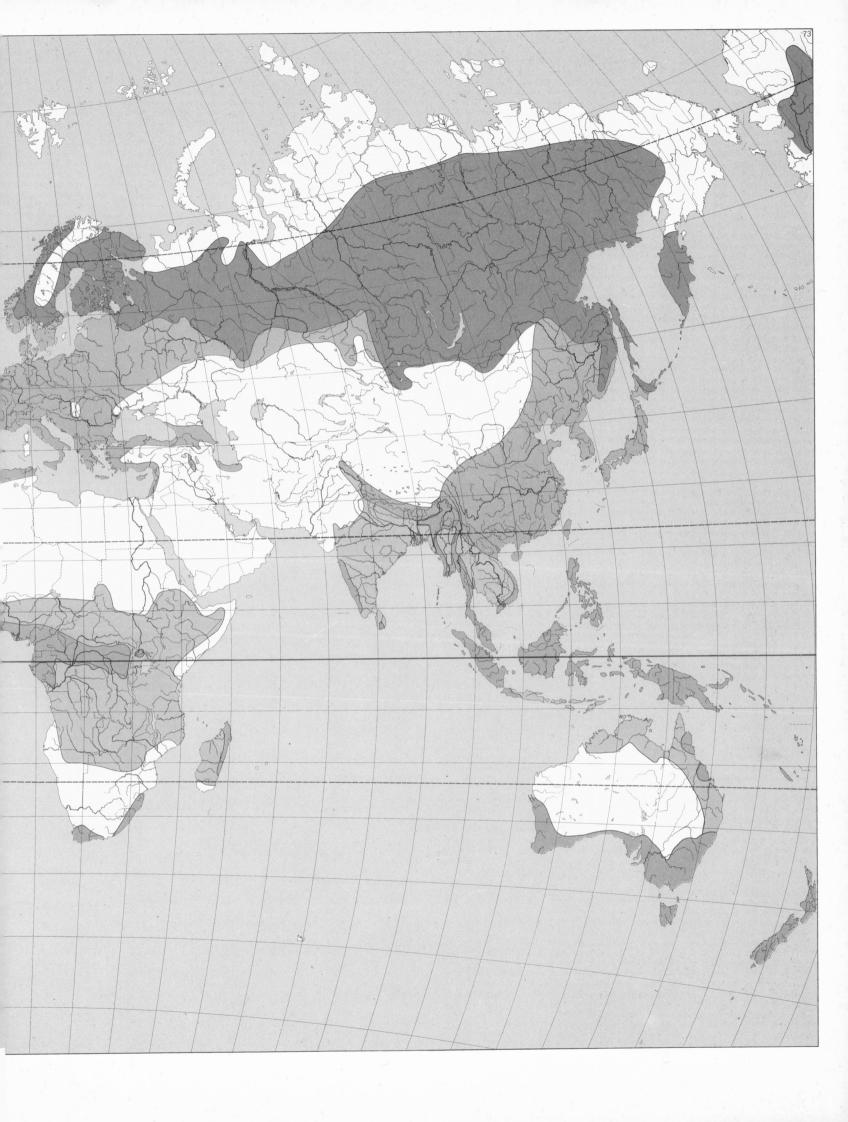

routes and extensive rubber plantations were soon laid out there, notably in Malaya. Nowadays, in the age of synthetic rubber, caoutchouc production from the primeval forests or plantations has lost much of its importance. Chewing gum, on the other hand, is still a natural product of the American naseberry tree, *Achras zapota*.

This tree also supplies very good and extremely durable timber which was used by the Maya Indians more than a thousand years ago for the construction of their magnificent temple and pyramid complexes in the rain forest of the Guatemalan lowlands and which has survived to this day in spite of the hot humid climate. Timber of the most varied characteristics, ranging from very light (the lightest in the world is that of the famous balsa tree) to the heaviest which instantly sinks in water, from purest white to black, dark purple, pink and scarlet, yellow and golden brown, in any conceivable grain and patterning–the rain forest produces such a vast variety of woods that nothing like a complete list of them exists to this day.

The trees of the rain forests are continually in blossom and in fruit, they continually shed their leaves and renew themselves since there is no unfavorable season ever to interrupt their growth or force them into dormancy. Nevertheless the rain forest is not a paradise, even for the plants. There is a ceaseless silent but merciless struggle for light among its denizens, and light means life. Any means that leads to victory is applied. Lianas climb into the highest crowns, rob the tree by which they have pulled themselves up of its sunlight, smother it and crush it pitilessly. The strangler fig germinates and grows in the fork of a branch where a handful of humus has accumulated. It sends its aerial roots downwards in the shape of thin threads, and once they have gained a foothold the host tree is doomed. Slowly and ruthlessly the fig first develops a kind of grid which gradually grows into a tube around the tree's stem which serves it as an indispensable support and then strangles it. For several decades the tree's corpse continues to serve as the core of the victorious fig tree. The strangler fig is perhaps the best known but not the only killer among the ligneous plants of the rain forest. In South America they are known as *matapalos*, "tree killers".

As we climb from the lowlands into the mountains the rain forests accompany us wherever the precipitation is sufficient to meet the high water requirements of its denizens. These mountain rain forests are also evergreen, but it should be pointed out that the green of the tropical forest is generally quite different from that of the European forest. The dominant colour is a rather pale dull green, touched with grey, rust-coloured to red and yellow tints. The tropical forest lacks the fresh brightness of the European broadleaved trees.

With rising altitude above sea level the composition and structure of the stands change. The giants with the massive plank buttresses disappear. The numerous *Leguminosae,* typical of the lowland rain forest, recede. Species of the laurel, rose and myrtle families become more numerous. But the wealth of tree species continues to be great–40 to 60 per hectare. The dominant trees reach a height of 65 to 130 feet; below their more or less compact canopy lies a second and a third storey. Lianas are less common but the number of epiphytes, including orchids and pineapple plants, increases.

Higher still, in the cloud or mist forests, the first primeval-looking tree ferns find their optimal living conditions. These magnificent forests owe their name to the fact that they are very frequently bathed in cloud and mist. Their zone covers the altitudes at which the vapour-saturated air rising from the hot humid lowlands condenses upon cooling. This process, even in fine weather, usually causes the formation of cloud banks in the condensation zone by early afternoon. The cloud forest, being a genuine rain forest, is evergreen and in spite of the cool climate still surprisingly rich in tree species–about 100 to 150. Among them for the first time we encounter some which are reminiscent of our familiar European trees. Thus in the cloud forests of the Venezualian Andes two species of cherries, a relation of the horse chestnut, a walnut species and tree-type hollies thrive, as well as alders and willows along the mountain streams. The most beautiful and richest cloud forests are dominated by conifers up to 130 feet tall, species of *Podocarpus,* distant relations of the European yew. This is also a favourite habitat of the cinchona tree whose bark contains the quinine that was used against malaria.

The cloud forest lacks trees with plank buttresses and there are no stem flowers. Lianas and creepers are fairly rare, and so are palms. Their place is taken, as already mentioned, by the large number of tree ferns up to 50 feet tall. The canopy is in three storeys but frequently the separate layers are difficult to distinguish. Everywhere one encounters magnificent large-blossomed orchids, numerous bromelias with brilliant red and yellow flower centers, delicate ornamental ferns, philodendrons, wild fuchsias and begonias.

Rain-green and dry forests in the tropics

The dry forest represents quite a different world. Wherever, within the tropical zone, the rainy periods are short while the annual dry periods last several months we find light low dry forests–provided the water is altogether sufficient for tree growth. Wherever and for whatever reasons trees grow on the limit of their viability potential we can always observe quite specific phenomena of adaptation to a hostile environment. We have already noted the fact in the case of the mangroves and we now find it again where

trees are struggling on the thirst line. In order to meet the threatening danger of death from lack of water they shed their leaves at the beginning of the dry season so that the dry forest stands bare for several
months each year. In this way evaporation and hence water consumption are drastically reduced. The
same purpose is served by the frequently observed reduction in leaf size. Many denizens of the dry forest
form small delicate, often multiple pinnate leaves. Particularly typical are a whole series of leguminosae
such as acacia, mimosa, mesquite and others which, moreover, are often distinguished by flat wide-
spreading crowns (umbrella-like acacia). Reduction can go so far that the leaves are partially or totally
transformed into thorns. This phenomenon is so frequent that certain formations of the dry forest are
rightly described as thorn forest or thorn scrub. Other species possess hard leathery leaves whose ana-
tomical construction ensures a very low transpiration.

Another extremely interesting adaptation to a precarious water budget is the ability to store water for
emergencies. A conspicuous example are the cactuses which we normally know only as pot plants. But
some representatives of this family can assume an entirely tree-shaped appearance and these are valued
highly as suppliers of wood in the poor dry zones; examples are *Peireskia guamacho* and *Cereus peruvi-
anus*. In Africa there are no cactuses; their place is taken by water-storing spurges (Euphorbiaceae), start-
lingly similar to cactuses in appearance but botanically belonging to quite different families.

Proper trees too are capable of storing water in their ligneous body (or more accurately, within the xylem ring). These water stores are often easily identified by the bottle or barrel-shaped swellings of the
stem which give the trees an odd and frequently an almost bizarre appearance. In South America they
are called *barrigones,* "pot bellies", or *palos borrachos,* "drunks", by the natives. Their crowns are
usually formed by a few thick ramified branches which further increase the impression of misshapenness
and awkwardness conveyed by these unusual trees. Professor Troll has appropriately called them the
"pachyderms of the forest".

A well-known pot-belly is the Ceiba tree, *Ceiba pentandra,* which is also commercially very valuable.
The fibres in which the seed is embedded supply kapok. The family of Bombacaceae also includes other
barrigones such as *Chorisia* and *Bombax* species. As well as the African baobab or monkey bread tree,
Adansonia digitata. Water storage can also take place in the leaves–commonly in agave and aloe species
–and below ground in the base of the stem or in the roots.

The far-ranging and deep root system of the dry forest trees similarly serves an improved water supply.
Since each individual tree requires an extensive root area to meet its moisture requirements the dry forest is an open forest. Incidentally, the shortage of water, intensified during the rainless months to a criti-

cal degree, is also the reason why the trees here only reach heights from about 26 to 50 feet and why the stands are single-storeyed. For the same reason also the dry forest is poor in species. Although we are still in the tropics there is nothing left to remind us of the luxuriance of the rain forest.

During the long dry months the dry forest appears dusty, bare and lifeless. But with the coming of the rains the trees are covered with green, and many are decked with blossoms of every conceivable shape and color. Life, flowering, growth and fruiting are compressed into a short span of time. Soon the leaves drop, soon the hard struggle is resumed for the few drops of water which are of vital importance to the survival of the dry forest.

There is an enormous gap between the rich rain forest and the poor dry forest. Between these two extremes are a great variety of communities which may be subsumed under the heading of rain-green tropical forests. They flourish in the periodically humid climatic zone within the tropics, shedding their leaves entirely or partially during the dry season and turning verdant again at the beginning of each rainy period. This distinguishes them from the evergreen rain forest. On the other hand the dry season here is less marked and also shorter than in the dry forest. Apart from shedding their leaves the rain-green tropical forests manage without special adaptation to aridity. Broadly speaking, they are subject to a similar seasonal rhythm as the European broadleaved trees: while in European latitudes this rhythm is governed by winter temperatures, in the tropical zones it is governed by periodical drought.

In contrast to the European forest trees, which are usually not very conspicuous in this respect, many species of the rain-green tropical forest are normally arrayed in magnificent blossoms towards the end of the dry season.

Overnight their still bare crowns turn into brilliant giant bunches of flowers. The trumpet trees (T. pentaphylla) produce pure golden yellow blooms, the crowns of the slender Cordia-alliodora trees stand brilliant white against the deep blue tropical sky, members of the Bombacaceae display large beautifully shaped white blossoms, as do also the balsa and the kapok tree, Bombacopsis quinta, and others; thousands of bright blue bells adorn the boughs of the jacaranda trees, and the coral trees (Erythrina spp.) are covered with brilliant red flames.

As a rule their splendor and that of many other species with fine flowers is rather short-lived. It is usually extinguished by the first heavy cloudbursts. The blossoms drop and the trees turn green.

In their leafy state the rain-green forests do not differ very greatly from the rain forest. On closer inspection it is found that they are differently composed and, with 30 to 50 tree species per hectare, are both poorer in species and less complex. The highest trees reach 80 to 115 feet, with diameters of about 6 feet. Palms are not as frequent in the upper storey; climbers and epiphytes are less in evidence. Stem-flowering trees and trees with pronounced plant buttresses are not entirely absent but are less numerous. The stems have only three storeys.

Much more interesting than the outward appearance of the trees, which by European standards would be described as normal, is the fact that the rain-green tropical forests contain many of the well-known tropical luxury and cabinet woods like the fashionable teak in Asia, true mahogany in Central and South America, okumé in Africa, palisander and ebony predominantly in Asia, and rosewood in Brazil.

This necessarily cursory glance at the confusing multiplicity of tree forms nevertheless reveals a common feature uniting the fir of the taiga, the primeval forest giant in the Congo, the Patagonian *Nothofagus,* the umbrella-like acacia under the scorching tropical sun, the sea-conquering mangroves, the exotic mahogany tree and our native oak with all other trees of the world, regardless of their differences–the harmony and beauty of natural creation and the powerful grandeur of living nature.

11 Aleppo pines *(Pinus halepensis)* on the island of Saint-
  Honorat in the Alpes Maritimes, France

12 Forests along the Ourthe in the Belgian Ardennes

13 The oak forest of Bellême, France

14 Bow River Valley in the Banff National Park, Alberta, Canada ▷

19 Japanese Kurile larches
  (Larix gmelini) with a bamboo species
  (Sasa shikotanensis)

20 Stilt roots (black mangrove, *Avicennia nitida*)

21 Bald cypresses *(Taxodium distichum)* in Louisiana, U.S.A.

24 Grand Canyon National Park, Arizona; trees fighting
   for survival against heat and drought

25 Palm forest *(Butia capitata)* in the Uruguayan pampas,
South America

26 Jungle clearance for agricultural use, Yucatan, Mexico

27 Road construction and lumbering, southern Sierra Madre, Mexico

28 Thunderclouds over Mount Rundle and Vermilion Lake, Alberta, Canada

29 Rocky Mountains National Park, Colorado, U.S.A.: Chasm Lake at the foot of Longs Peak

32 A *troika*, the traditional three-horse sleigh in a Siberian forest, U.S.S.R.

33 Threatened forest edge region in the North

35 Timber floating on the Mana River, Krasnoyarsk region, U.S.S.R.

36 Spruce woods of the same age *(Picea abies)* ▷

37 Winter in a Finnish forest ▷▷

38 In a continuous-succession forest the airspace is filled with green leaves ▷▷▷

Species of Trees

Enrique Marcet

As early as the Palaeozoic the first tree-type plants with tall crowned stems formed extensive forest-like vegetation types. The first peak in forest development on earth is undoubtedly represented by the forests of the Carboniferous period, some 280 million years ago, with mighty Lycopodium trees, such as the 30 foot high *Sigillaria* or the 100 foot high and six foot thick scale trees, *Lepidodendron,* as well as *Calamites* growing to over 30 feet. All that survives of these colossal spore-bearing plants from that primeval age are their low-growing relations; their part in forest formation has been taken over by modern flower and seed-bearing timbers which have evolved from simple forms in the course of millions of years. These are essentially the gymnospermous conifers, whose beginnings go back a good 200 million years, and the angiospermous broadleaved trees which did not originate until later.

Coniferous and broadleaved trees

The conifers are nowadays represented in the world by more than 500 species, principally in the northern temperate zone. They are characterized by the naked ovules of the female flowers, not enclosed by *carpophylls*; the flowers as a rule are arranged in cone-shaped inflorescences which subsequently grow into lignified seed clusters, the cones. Only a few species, such as the yew and the juniper, have different cone formations, of stone fruit or berry type. The needle or scale-shaped leaf organs, with the exception of four species, are evergreen. Only the larch, the golden larch *(Pseudolarix),* the swamp cypress *(Taxodium,* also known as the bald cypress), and the prehistoric dawn redwood *(Metasequoia),* discovered in China as recently as 1947, are bare in winter. The stem of coniferous forests as a rule is very straight and continuous to the top; this can be seen particularly clearly with spruces and firs. The branches are arranged regularly and, with the exception of, for instance, yew and larch, predominantly in whorls as a result of a whorl arrangement of the buds.

The broadleaved trees with their far more numerous species differ from the conifers mainly by their ovules being enclosed within an ovary, and by the formation of a fruit. As the pollen can no longer directly reach the ovules a special receptive organ, the stigma, has been developed on the ovary. In regions with cold winters and in some periodically hot dry regions the leaves are shed during the unfavourable season; in warm humid regions the trees are evergreen. The stem of broadleaved trees as a rule is less straight than that of conifers and branching is also less regular.

Growth and age

The various species of forest trees differ greatly in their economic importance. An essential aspect of this is not only the quality of the timber–although this, of course, is decisive–but also the growth rate and tree size. Although under optimal conditions any tree will grow particularly well, considerable differences nevertheless exist even under comparable conditions. Thus oaks and, more particularly, yews grow only slowly compared with, say, poplars or willows. While the former reach their commercial cutting maturity in 150 years at the earliest, fast-growing cultivated poplars can be cut at 20 to 30 years, and even earlier in climatically favoured regions such as the Po plain in Italy where six-year-old poplars can reach a diameter of up to 12 inches. Faster growing still are the South American balsa and Australian eucalyptus species which are nowadays planted not only in their native country but throughout the warm regions.

An even more striking difference exists between different tree species when we look at their size. Yew, Arolla pine, hornbeam and maple achieve only modest height–at best 65 feet. By comparison with these trees of a slight order of magnitude spruces and firs represent veritable giants: they are capable over the centuries of reaching 165 to 200 feet with diameters of about 6 feet. A particularly well-known example is the Dürsrüti fir which was felled at Langnau in the Swiss Emmental in 1947 at an age of 320 years; this had grown to a height of 174 feet with a diameter of over 6 feet and a trunk volume of 989 cubic feet. Larches, too, occasionally surpass 165 feet, but the tallest broadleaved trees such as the common oak, beech, elm, summer lime and ash attain, at best, 130 feet or slightly more. However, the stateliest European spruces and firs are still dwarfed by the real giants of this earth, which are well over twice their height and which grow, not as might be expected in the tropical rain forest but in the Australian savannas and in the coniferous forest zone of the North American West. Whereas in the former regions these giants are exclusively broadleaved trees (Eucalyptus species) which can reach heights of nearly 400 feet, for instance *Eucalyptus regnans,* the latter regions contain the conifers with the greatest height and diameters so far registered. A record height of 427 feet was measured on a coastal sequoia in California, the so-called redwood, *Sequoia sempervirens;* but even Douglas fir, *Pseudotsuga menziesii,* can here attain 417 feet and Sitka pine, *Picea sitcensis,* about 330 feet. The west American giants topping 262 feet further include the giant fir, *Abies grandis,* the sugar or Lambert's pine, *Pinus lambertiana,* the western hemlock, *Tsuga heterophylla,* the giant arborvitae, *Thuja plicata,* and of course the giant sequoia or big tree, *Sequoiadendron giganteum,* although this owes its fame more to its girth and age than its height. Whereas the redwoods achieve a diameter of "only" 20 feet, the thickest giant sequoia in the Californian Sierra Nevada has a diameter of 39 feet and an overall height of 272 feet. At 180 feet above ground its stem still is over 13 feet across; its biggest branch has a length of 141 feet and a diameter of 6 feet. Its total trunk volume amounts to 49,500 cubic feet, approximately the amount of standing timber on over 22 acres of average California pine forest and more timber than on 2.5 acres of the best-stocked Emmental selection-system forest in Switzerland. A church seating 300, complete with a 65-foot steeple, was once built from the trunk of a single giant sequoia. Today the giant sequoias are protected over a total area of 2,495 square miles which at present still contains roughly 20,000 trees of a diameter in excess of 10 feet.

Needless to say, even fast-growing species can attain such dimensions only over very considerable periods of time, and indeed some of these western American giants are veritable Methuselahs. A ring count of one such felled giant sequoia showed it to be 3,212 years old. Its early youth, therefore, must have been roughly at the time of Moses's exodus from Egypt. The age of the biggest individuals is estimated at 3,500 to 4,000 years. Yet there are older trees still. A surprise was caused in the White Mountains of California in 1954 by the discovery that some quite insignificant and exceedingly slow-growing bristlecone pines, *Pinus aristata,* showed up to 4,600 annual growth rings. Their long life, therefore, began when the Egyptians were building their pyramids. By comparison the life-span of European tree species is quite modest, with aspens, willows, alders and birches seldom exceeding 150 years.

Flowers and propagation

Only slightly less varied than their appearance, growth rate or life-span are the phenomena displayed by different trees with regard to their propagation.

To begin with, different tree species reach sexual maturity at widely differing ages. Whereas poplars, willows, birches and alders form flowers within their first ten years, firs, beeches and oaks do not reach maturity until they are 50 to 80 years old. However, the age of flower formation may be greatly affected by certain environmental influences. Thus sexual maturity occurs substantially earlier in solitary trees growing freely than in those forming part of a forest where their crowns cannot develop to the full. Likewise, early maturity can be promoted by poor soils. Finally suitable artificial measures such as ringing, strangulation or root pruning can achieve earlier or particularly plentiful flower development; this may be desirable for arboricultural purposes or with an eye to heavy seed production, but not when maximum timber production is aimed at.

Different arrangements are found also in our forest trees with regard to the distribution of the two flower sexes. Thus there are mixed-sex, so-called monoecious, species in which the flowers of both sexes are formed on the same individual. In this case the male and female organs may either be united in a hermaphroditic flower, as for instance in lime, bird cherry and robinia, or they are arranged on separate single-sex flowers, as for instance in birch, alder, beech, hornbeam, oak, spruce, fir, larch and pine. By way of contrast the so-called dioecious species have their male and female flowers shared out between separate individuals. Certain individuals of poplar, willow, yew, juniper or ash-leaf maple (box elder) therefore carry only male or only female flowers.

In most forest trees the pollen is transferred to the female flowers not by insects or other animals but by the wind. These species display certain characteristics which testify to a special adaptation to wind pollination, such as tall growth, occurrence in massive stands, and above all the organization of flowers which are usually united into dense inflorescences. Thus the wind-pollinated broadleaved trees like oak, poplar, hornbeam, walnut, alder, birch and beech possess pendent male flowers which can move in the wind and from which the pollen can easily be blown out or shaken out, whereas the female flowers are equipped with large thread or brush-shaped stigmas to facilitate adhesion of the wind-borne pollen. Wind-pollinated broadleaved species also frequently blossom early in the spring, i.e. before or at the beginning of leaf formation so that the dispersal of the pollen is obstructed as little as possible by the foliage. As for the conifers, the needles are less of an obstacle and, besides, the male flowers usually occur towards the ends of the shoots so that later flowering represents no handicap. Owing to the minute size and exiguous weight of the individual pollen grains the pollen of wind-fertilized tree species are very readily airborne. Thus a grain of beech pollen measures only about 0.0035 mm and weighs 0.000018 grams. During the day the light pollen is carried high up above the tree-tops by thermal up-currents; considerable quantities of it have been shown by aircraft to be present at heights of up to 10,000 feet. Overnight it slowly sinks to the ground–spruce pollen, for instance, at an average settling speed of 6 cm and juniper pollen at only 0.9 cm per second. Enormous quantities of pollen are produced each year, especially in the large coniferous regions, a fact which is sometimes impressively demonstrated by the well-known "sulfur rain" after heavy downpours. Experiments conducted in the surroundings of Zurich revealed a precipitation of 20,531 grains of tree pollen per square centimeter in 1950, corresponding to a pollen mass of about 40 lbs. per acre (50 kg per hectare). The tree pollen is carried not only to a great altitude but also over very considerable horizontal distances. Thus oak pollen has been trapped on the island of Helgoland, blown from the mainland over a distance of 37 to 44 miles. The absolute limit of pollen dispersal exceeds 1,250 miles.

A subordinate role to wind pollination, at least in European forests, is played by pollen transfer by animals. In these latitudes it is chiefly insects, such as hymenoptera, diptera, butterflies and beetles, while in the tropics certain trees are pollinated also by birds and bats. Pure insect-pollinated trees in European forests are willow and lime, bird cherry and mountain ash, as well as robinia or pseudo-acacia, originally a native of North America but long established in Europe. By comparison with the rather haphazard and wasteful wind pollination, pollination by insects is much more economical and in a certain sense controlled, especially if performed by bees which, as is known, possess a highly developed ability to communicate and are also very consistent as to flowers and sites visited. Finally, the very nature of the individual pollen grain is purposefully adapted to propagation by insects: it contains oily adhesive substances which ensure both clotting of the grains amongst each other and good adhesion to the hair cover of the insects. The same purpose is served also by the frequently almost "baroque" sculpture of the pollen grain.

The female flowers of our forest trees are not as a rule fertilized by pollen from the same tree but through cross-pollination. In the case of dioecious species, such as the poplar, willow, juniper and yew, this seems obvious since the two sexes are not found on the same tree. But even certain monoecious tree species must be fertilized by pollen from other trees of the same species whenever the two sex organs do not flower simultaneously, as is the case with lime, ash and mountain ash, or in the case of self-sterility, i.e. when the female organs are not receptive to the pollen of the same tree. This applies very largely to oak and Spanish chestnut. European spruces, firs, larches and pines, on the other hand, show a certain self-fertility although the poorly germinating seeds only produce seedlings of low vitality. Entirely self-fertile, on the other hand, are the alders, the hornbeam and the walnut, and among conifers the Serbian spruce from the Balkans, *Picea omorica,* which is frequently planted as an ornamental tree.

Fertilization proper, the union of the sperm nucleus of the pollen with the ovum of the female flower, takes place several weeks after pollination in the case of broadleaved trees, as well as in spruce and larch, and after as much as a year in the case of pine. In consequence, the cones and seeds of pine species ripen roughly towards the end of the second year. Certain oak species likewise require two years for fructification, such as the South European Austrian or Turkey oak, *Quercus cerris,* the Mediterranean ilex or holm oak, *Quercus ilex,* the cork oak, *Quercus suber,* as well as the North American red oak *Quercus borealis,* which enjoys hospitality in European forests. By contrast the acorns of Central European species invariably ripen in a single year. As for shape and size of fruits, cones and seeds, the various tree species display a surprising variety. Among all native European forest trees the aspen and silky sand willow have the smallest seeds. They are barely 1 mm long and one thousand of them only weigh about 100 milligrams. Nevertheless, within a few decades, trees grow from them to a height of 100 feet. Such trees, therefore, do not necessarily produce large fruits or seeds. Even the sequoias, the biggest trees in the world, only have cones the length of a chicken egg and very flat seeds only 3 to 4 mm big. The most massive giant sequoia today, with its 544 tons, weighs 58 million million times as much as the seed from which it has sprung. Other tree species form large and heavy seeds, such as the oak, the walnut, the Spanish chestnut and the Arolla pine. One thousand acorns, for example, weigh 6 to 10 lbs. (3–5 kg). The cones of various coniferous species can similarly display considerable differences in size. The American arborvitae carries only minute cones, barely 1 cm long, while the West American Lambert's pine, *Pinus lambertiana,* carries cones up to 60 cm (2 feet) long. From the same region comes the big-cone pine, *Pinus coulteri,* whose monstrous spiky cones weigh up to 5 lbs. (2.5 kg) in their green state and are not without good cause known as "widow-makers". Some cones, such as those of the spruce, having shed their seeds, drop to the ground whole, while fir or cedar cones begin to break up on the tree. With a few pine species, on the other hand, such as the North American jack pine *Pinus banksiana,* and especially the knob-cone pine, *Pinus attenuata,* the ripe cones remain closed for up to 20 years before they are eventually forced by the heat of a forest fire to open their scales and release the seeds. The small-seed species like poplar, willow, birch and alder produce quite prodigious quantities of seed each year but invariably only a small percentage encounters conditions favouring germination. Even the small seedlings are still exceedingly vulnerable and very sensitive to drought. Although a large, fully grown aspen produces several million seeds each year, successful natural rejuvenation is rarely observed. It has also been calculated that in the course of 28 years one birch with all its issue would produce enough seeds to re-forest the entire dry surface of the earth. Obviously, by way of contrast, the large-seed species must be far more economical in their seed production as this uses up a great many nutritive substances which are then lost to timber production. Even with conifers producing only medium-weight seed between 18 and 28 cubic feet of timber can be lost per acre in this manner in a seed-rich year. The heavy-seed species produce major quantities of seed only every few years and can thus recover during the intervening period. The walnut, for instance, has a pronounced seed year roughly every three years, the oak every four or five years, and the beech every five to eight years. In cooler conditions the intervals are even longer. The conifers show an analogous rhythm; thus fir and pine of two to four years, spruce of three to eight years, while the Arolla pine as a pronounced mountain tree only provides its "nuts" on a more generous scale every six to fifteen years.

Small and light seeds are normally propagated by the wind, a method for which they are suitably equipped in a variety of ways–either by means of minute hair tufts, as the seeds of poplar or willow, or by means of wings of different types of construction, such as the rotary-winged seeds of spruce, fir, pine, larch, maple, ash, hornbeam and lime, or the sail-winged seeds of elm, birch, and white and alpine alder. The large seeds of walnut, beech, oak, Spanish chestnut and Arolla pine, on the other hand, are not capable of flight and are propagated as a rule by seed-transporting animals such as mice, squirrels, jays and wood pigeons. The seeds of the yew, juniper, wild cherry and mountain ash are propagated by berry-feeding birds. The seeds of the black alder, with its preferred site by the water, are adapted to water propagation by floating pads. In addition to sexual propagation, characterized by pollination, fertilization and seed formation, some tree species possess the ability of asexual or vegetative propagation: their roots develop suckers which, after the death of the parent tree, grow up into independent trees. This so-called root breeding is found in particular with the aspens, the white alder and the mountain ash. Spruces in the mountains also develop roots from their lowest branches, which lie on the ground, and this enables them, even after the death of the parent tree, to survive on their own and erect themselves as trees. Such "shoots" occur frequently also with fallen poplars, willows and other broadleaved trees. Agriculture and forestry, as well as horticulture, have long utilized this property of certain plants and moreover developed further artificial methods of vegetative propagation, such as propagation by cuttings and of strain improvement by grafting. Thus potatoes, fruit trees, date palms, sugar cane, banana and fig trees, as well as sharp-leaved triandrous willows and cultured poplars are propagated exclusively by the vegetative method. In this way valuable types may be preserved at will with their hereditary properties and multiplied on a large scale with "consistent quality". The broadleaved underforest also rejuvenates itself vegetatively with the stumps of felled trees sending up shoots which in turn grow into trees.

An important difference between the two types of propagation is the circumstance that in sexual propagation the genetic stock of the two partners is blended, which may lead to the emergence of new and possibly favorable combinations of qualities, whereas in the case of asexual propagation only a certain part of the parent tree grows into an independently viable plant with the maternal genetic endowment. Sexual propagation therefore safeguards the continuous development of the species while vegetative propagation does not produce any new combinations.

Climate and site requirements

Less conspicuous but certainly no less varied are, finally, the particular demands which the various tree species make on their environment, principally on climate and soil. Knowledge of these site requirements is one of the most important conditions for the successful economic management of trees and forests. A decisive factor, to start with, is warmth since it is this which renders possible the most important vital functions of the trees and also determines the limit of their distribution both in the North and in the mountains. To demonstrate the marked difference between the requirements of warmth of one tree species and another we do not have to compare tropical and northern species; even within our domestic tree flora we find substantial differences. Generally speaking, a forest can still thrive where the average temperature throughout at least 60 days in the year amounts to about 50°F (10°C). Certain tree species are often content with less, such as the extremely undemanding mountain pine which in the Alps can manage with a vegetative period of only four to six weeks. By way of contrast the common oak requires at least 54°F (12°C) for four to nine months. The walnut is even more demanding.

Species like yew, fir, and common elm are sensitive to winter cold whereas the spruce along the Siberian tree line tolerates winter frosts of −76°F (−60°C). Birches, aspens and pines can likewise tolerate low winter temperatures just as well as great summer heat. Naturally all these species are considerably more sensitive during their vegetative period than during winter dormancy, which is why autumn or spring frosts usually cause greater damage than low temperatures in winter. Thus the Mediterranean evergreen ilex can survive temperatures of down to 10°F (−12°C) in winter while during its vegetation period temperatures of 43 to 45°F (+6°C to 7°C) can be dangerous to it.

Considerable differences are also found in the amount of water required by the various tree species. Thus the undemanding pine manages to thrive on rocky knolls or on the edge of the southern Russian steppes with an annual precipitation of only 400 mm (under 16 inches) whereas black alder, black poplar and silky sand willow need a lot of water and therefore prefer sites at the water's edge. This difference in water requirement is reflected also in the quantity needed by different tree species to produce 1 kg (2.2 lbs.) of dry wood mass: for this the pine uses 180 liters (about 40 English or 48 U.S. gallons) while the poplar needs 500 liters (110 English or 122 U.S. gallons). It is not surprising that from such moisture-demanding species as the poplar large quantities of water are also evaporated. It has been calculated that the leaves of a poplar stand of 1 hectare (2.5 acres) can give off more than 50,000 liters (11,000 English or 12,000 U.S. gallons) of evaporated water into the atmosphere during a 24 hour period.

As with all green plants, the main source of energy for our forest trees is sunlight; with its help the chlorophyll produces the substances needed for building up the massive timber body. The growth of a tree, fundamentally, is nothing other than a ceaseless striving for light, of which apparently it can never have enough. Yet there are also considerable variations in the amount of light demanded by different tree species–a circumstance acknowledged by the silvicultural distinction between light and shade-loving species. Extremely light-demanding trees are pine, larch, birch and poplar, which do not tolerate any constriction of their crowns and scarcely any shading by spreading branches of other trees. In contrast to these light-loving trees the box tree and the yew are able to survive the deepest shade of all native European species. But fir and beech are also pronouncedly shade-loving and can endure many decades deep inside dark stands. Individuals especially dependent on light, such as the pine, are often prepared to make drastic concessions in order to meet their high demand for light. Wherever they are too hard pressed by shading species they retreat even to poor dry sites where the more demanding tree species no longer thrive. Others, as for instance, the mountain pine or the common birch move into marshland where their rivals cannot follow them. Many light-loving species tolerate rather more shade in their earliest youth than in old age; this is because seedling establishment is normally under the cover of the parent stand or in gaps in the stand with lateral shading. Shade-loving trees, on the other hand, require a little more light in old age. The demand for light can also be somewhat modified by the soil: on nutritious and sufficiently irrigated forest soil most tree species tolerate more shade than on greatly desiccated and impoverished soil.

Our blanket references to tree species may have conveyed the impression that these are in each case a large number of trees of identical appearance and identical living habits. But especially on this latter point there are scarcely any two trees which behave identically, provided of course we are not dealing with vegetative propagation. Let us consider the pine which has a vast area of distribution, reaching from the Spanish Sierra Nevada at 40° Northern latitude to the tree line 30° further to the North, and from Scotland far into Northern Asia. If we now tried to transplant Spanish pines to Sweden or Scottish pines to Siberia, or vice versa, these plantations in all four localities would fail utterly because the trees are closely associated with the climate of their place of origin and cannot without grave consequences be transported into substantially different environments. They are the products of a natural selection over thousands of years under definite climatic conditions, and that is also why their adaptive capacity is part of their genetic equipment. The tree species as a whole have become differentiated, under the effect of diverse climates, into different climatic races. Definite races of tree species are particularly adapted to the duration of the vegetative period, the prevailing winter temperatures, to low humidity, or to a particular length of daylight during the vegetative period, and for this reason North European tree races do not thrive well in Southern Europe.

The fact that representatives of the same tree species may show very divergent behavior is of enormous importance to forestry. A thorough knowledge not only of the demands and habits of the various species, but also of the genetically conditioned variability within a species, enables the experienced silviculturalist to build up a permanently profitable and resistant commercial forest in harmony with all factors of the local environment.

European and North American tree flora

In connection with the environmental demands of tree species we have seen that temperature is an essential condition of plant life. It is therefore not surprising that we should find a larger number of different plants, including tree species, in the warmer regions of the earth than in the cooler ones. However, striking differences in the number of native tree species are found to exist also between entirely comparable regions. Thus, compared with North America the tree flora of Europe is poor in species. Whereas Cis-alpine Europe has only some 50 tree species, Canada has about 150 and the U.S.A. as many as 850 including numerous species not represented in Europe even by related ones. Thus, Europe has only one species of spruce as against seven in the U.S.A.: the ratio for firs is one to nine, for pines three to thirty-five, and for oaks three to at least sixty.

The explanation of this strange phenomenon must be sought in the most recent chapter of geological history. About a million years ago the European and North American floras under the then prevailing sub-tropical climate were very similarly composed. Numerous species growing in North America were also represented in Europe at that time and many of these can still be traced in fossils in tertiary strata. The sequoia advanced from Italy as far as Spitsbergen and its timber, together with that of the deciduous or bald cypress, *Taxodium,* supplies our brown coal. Other species then flourishing in Europe were magnolia and tulip trees, horse chestnuts, hickory species and plane trees.

During the Ice Age the average temperature in Europe dropped by about 18° F (10° C) so that those warmth-loving species which did not succeed in emigrating in time to regions more favorable to vegetation died out. But the Ice Age as such was not the main cause of impoverishment of the European tree flora; North America, too, experienced its Ice Age with three times as much land glaciated as in Europe. The decisive factor was that the European mountain ranges like the Pyrenees, the Alps, the Bohemian Forest, the Ore Mountains, the Sudeten, the Carpathians, the Balkans and the Caucasus run in an east-westerly direction, thus representing massive barriers which not only obstructed or blocked the way to the plants fleeing southward from the cold but also to the post-glacial re-immigrants. In North America, on the other hand, this process was associated with far fewer losses to the flora because escape to the south and return after the glaciation were easier. Europe thus owes its poverty of tree species to a geological accident. If therefore European forestry experts are now endeavouring to enrich their forests mainly with suitable North American tree species this is not a falsification of the native European tree flora since the ancestors of the imported trees were once naturally domiciled in Europe.

The first attempts at planting exotic tree species in Europe were made as long as 200 years or more ago, for aesthetic reasons or as a hobby. Very soon the biological advantages were realized, as well as the often associated greater viability of the exotic species, and experimental commercial plantations were started.

Systematic experimental planting of foreign species began in Germany about 1880 so that it is possible by now to judge the commercial suitability of a whole series of species. Some of them have in fact been systematically used for afforestation for several decades. The most widespread of these so far is the green Douglas fir, *Pseudotsuga taxifolia B., var. viridis.* The area planted to this tree in Germany is estimated at over 1,250,000 acres. It comes from the Western coastal regions of the U.S.A., where it attains a height of up to 190 feet. Its needles are softer than those of the fir and spruce, and if they are crushed between the fingers they give off a characteristic smell of turpentine.

Among foreign broadleaved trees one that is much planted in Europe is the red oak, *Quercus borealis M.,* native to the Eastern U.S.A. and Canada around the Great Lakes, chiefly because it grows more rapidly in its youth than do the European oaks and makes lesser demands on warm climate, water supply and nutritive content of the soil. It owes its name not only to the red coloration of its much favored autumnal foliage but also to the reddish hue of its wood, although this is not judged to be up to the quality of European veneer oak. Other conifers from the U.S.A. planted in Europe, in addition to the Douglas fir, are the Weymouth pine, *Pinus strobus L.,* which has a light soft wood but suffers from a rust fungus *(Peridermium strobi K.),* a number of other *Pinus* and *Abies* species, as well as the giant arborvitae *(Thuja plicata D.),* the Western hemlock *(Tsuga heterophylla S.)* and the big tree or giant sequoia *(Sequoia gigantea D.).*

Broadleaved trees native to the U.S.A. and planted in Europe include, in addition to the red oak, the tulip tree *(Liriodendron tulipifera N.);* experimental planting of maple, birch, walnut and plane species is being recommended.

Some well-known exotics come from other parts of the world, as, for instance, the Japanese larch *(Larix leptolepis G.)* from Hondo Island. In line with the climate of its homeland it needs a sufficiently humid atmosphere and will then grow more rapidly than the European larch *(Larix decidua M.).* It differs from it by the reddish coloring of its year-old shoots.

In Southern European countries, where there are no frosts, eucalyptus trees, in particular the blue eucalyptus or blue gum *(Eucalyptus globulus L.),* have lately been planted. There are nearly 200 species of these whose principal distribution area embraces Australia and the islands as far as the Philippines. The eucalyptus trees are among the world's tallest. Their rapid growth in youth often surpasses that of hybrid poplars. These are mostly crosses between American and European black poplars and may be regarded as the first cultured plants among forest trees.

40 Coastal redwoods *(Sequoia sempervirens)* in the Redwood Forest, California

41 Root system of beech

44 Elk's-horn fern *(Platycerium alcicorne)* growing as an epiphyte on a tree trunk

45 Strangler fig twining around an oak stem in the Everglades rain forest, Florida

53 Grove of edible chestnut *(Castanea sativa)* in the Ticino, Switzerland

54 Cypress grove *(Cupressus sempervirens)* in Corfu

55 Tree growth affected by wind,
Tierra del Fuego

56 Petrified tree stump in Syria ▷
57 Tropical forest clearing at sunset ▷▷

Structure and Growth of Wood

Heinrich Bosshard

Wood is one of the oldest raw materials used by man. It has served him as a source of heat and shelter, as cradle and coffin, as a tool of civilization and as a weapon. The story of the utilization of wood thus becomes part of the history of mankind; the wood age dates back to the very first periods of human existence and will continue far into the future. The secret of the constant position occupied by wood in our everyday lives lies in its adaptability and in its morphological, chemical and technological variety. A mere glance at the Earth's forest cover reveals the wide range of wood. Each species of tree or shrub has its own specifically structured wood body, and just as a dendrologist categorizes tree species according to their flowers, leaves and the shapes of shoots and buds, the wood anatomist can group the different kinds of wood according to cell type and arrangement, tissue structure and other typical aspects of minute structure.

The main division among lignified plants distinguishes between coniferous and broadleaved species. The obvious outward differences between them, in the shape of stem and foliage, are matched by differences in their wood structure: the simple severity of the structure of conifers is reflected in the somewhat archaic minute structure of their wood which contrasts markedly with that of the broadleaves. This is readily revealed by an examination of the cells involved in the wood structure. Dominant in coniferous wood (Plate 65A) are tracheids closed at both ends, accounting on an average for 95 per cent of the cells. The infinitely variegated wood structure of broadleaves is made possible by the numerous types of vessels, fibers, medullar ray cells and parenchyma strand cells (Plate 66a).

The two types of trees also have a great deal in common. Thus the cells of conifers and of broadleaves both originate in a tissue known as the cambium which lies between the wood and the bark (Plate 65B). The term cambium is derived from the Italian *cambiare* "to engage in trade exchange", since the cambium on one side produces the wood (xylem) and on the other the bark (phloem). The cambium thus becomes the most important tissue layer for tree growth. All external influences on the cambium–the rhythm of climatic change, frost or heat, injury or especially favorable conditions due to silvicultural care–and equally all internal regularities, are reflected in the structure of the wood. The wood thus becomes a record of cambial activity; from it may be read cambium's growth characteristics and vitality. Our oldest witnesses to date are the bristlecone pines of Arizona; in them the cambium has survived more than four thousand years, and there is no reason to suppose that this endurance is subject to any time limit. The secret of this timelessness of the cambium lies in the continual self-renewal of its fusiform and ray initials. Descended from fusiform initials, the axially oriented cells found in conifers produce longitudinal tracheids, parenchyma strand and epithelial cells; in broadleaves these cells produce vessels, tracheids, fibers and parenchyma strand cells. Ray initials produce such transverse elements as ray

Diagram 1

Cross section [CS]   Radial section [RS]   Tangential section [TS]

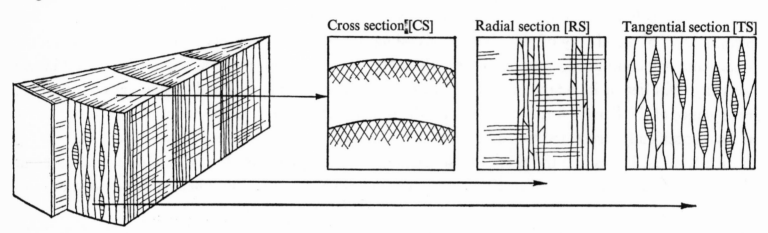

Softwood

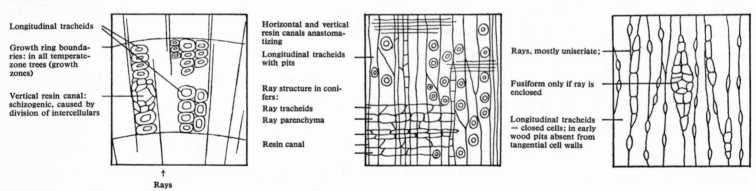

Longitudinal tracheids

Growth ring boundaries: in all temperate-zone trees (growth zones)

Vertical resin canal: schizogenic, caused by division of intercellulars

↑
Rays

Horizontal and vertical resin canals anastomatizing

Longitudinal tracheids with pits

Ray structure in conifers:

Ray tracheids

Ray parenchyma

Resin canal

Rays, mostly uniseriate;

Fusiform only if ray is enclosed

Longitudinal tracheids = closed cells; in early wood pits absent from tangential cell walls

Hardwood

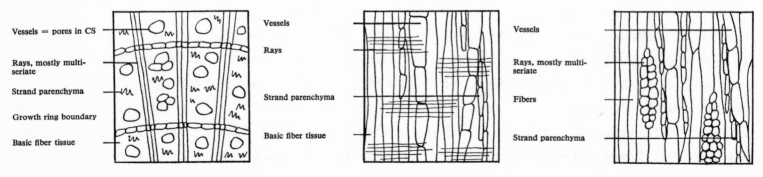

Vessels = pores in CS

Rays, mostly multiseriate

Strand parenchyma

Growth ring boundary

Basic fiber tissue

Vessels

Rays

Strand parenchyma

Basic fiber tissue

Vessels

Rays, mostly multiseriate

Fibers

Strand parenchyma

Diagram 2

Strand parenchyma arrangement and distribution in European broadleaves. Growth ring boundaries, pores, rays and strand parenchyma are shown (shaded) in the schematic cross sections.

Apotracheal distribution: Strand parenchyma not in close contact with the vascular system

Paratracheal distribution: Strand parenchyma in close contact with the vascular system

Betula

Populus

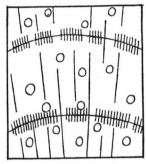

Robinia

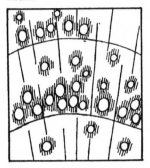

Ulmus

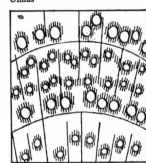

apotracheal diffuse
Strand parenchyma in CS irregularly embedded in the basic fiber tissue

apotracheal bands
Strand parenchyma mostly in fine bands: either at the beginning (initial) or the end (terminal) of the growth rings

paratracheal vasicentric
Vessels surrounded by strand parenchyma; the parenchyma sheath can have aliform widenings in tangential direction (aliform parenchyma)

paratracheal banded
Strand parenchyma in more or less broad bands between the vessels

tracheids, ray parenchyma cells and radially oriented epithelial cells in conifers, and ray parenchyma in broadleaves.

Wood therefore contains two intersecting cell systems. In order to examine these elements, as they combine in the tissue, wood samples have to be cut along three planes, as shown in Diagram 1: at right angles to the stem axis (transverse section), along the stem axis and parallel to the radial rays (radial section) and along the stem axis and tangentially to the annual rings (tangential section). These three sections through the wood make it possible to examine the varied interlocking of individual cells.

In all woods from the temperate zones the structure follows the general vegetational rhythm, marked by annual or growth rings. This is seen particularly clearly in the transverse section, where the early wood formed at the beginning of the vegetative period as a rule shows a looser structural type than the late wood in the remaining part of the growth ring. The transverse section also clearly displays the differences between softwood and hardwood (Diagram 1). With softwood the basic tissue formed by longitudinal tracheids is broken, in an axial direction, by at most a few axially ascending resin canals (Plate 65 B, C); in the wood of broadleaves numerous vessels pierce the basic fibrous tissue and, in transverse section, form more or less large pores (Plate 66 b, c, d). According to the arrangement of these pores in relation to the growth ring boundary and according to their size, one speaks of ring-porous (Plate 66 b–oak), diffuse-porous (Plate 66 c–poplar) and semi-ring-porous (Plate 66 d–cherry) woods. Other axial cell elements,

Diagram 3

Characteristics of bordered pit pairs. A cross section through the pit shows intracellular layers and primary wall (pit membrane) with torus, together with the fork-like arch of the secondary membranes. A radial section of a pit merely shows the outer contours of the pit border and the torus, together with the centrally situated porus.

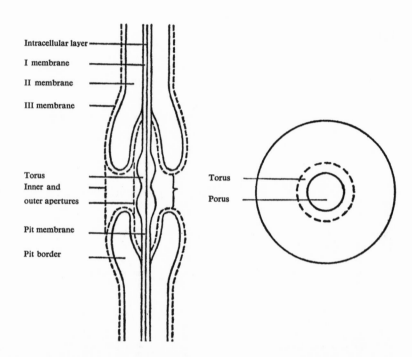

Intracellular layer

I membrane

II membrane

III membrane

Torus
Inner and
outer apertures

Pit membrane

Pit border

Torus

Porus

apart from tracheids, fibers and vessels, are the parenchyma strand cells. In softwood, admittedly, these occur only sparsely and usually accompany vertical resin canals; in the wood of broadleaves, on the other hand, they usually predominate. The distribution of these parenchyma strands in hardwood follows its own laws. As can be seen from Diagram 2 or from Plate 66r–u, in the apotracheal distribution type the parenchyma strand is in not very close contact with the vascular system, whereas in the paratracheal distribution type the parenchyma strand cells are grouped around the vessels. In further basic patterns of parenchyma arrangement, we distinguish between diffuse parenchyma (Plate 66r–oak), vasicentric parenchyma (Plate 66s–ebony), aliform parenchyma (Plate 66t–Pterocarpus) and banded parenchyma (Plate 66u–Shorea). These variants can be differentiated still further, but wood in fact normally contains combinations of parenchyma patterns.

The transverse section is made at right angles to the stem axis; hence revealing the full length of the rays which lie transversely in the tree, as shown in Diagram 1 and Plates 65D and 66d. In this plane the radially oriented rays in softwood appear as narrow bands, usually just one cell wide, whereas those in hardwood frequently appear as multiple bands more or less at right angles to the growth ring boundary. In conifers transversally oriented resin canals may be embedded in the rays; hence the two directions intersect and are in close contact. If, for instance, a resin-conducting ray is ruptured in the cambial zone through excessive external load, the resin not just from this canal but from the resin canal system over a wide area will collect in this laceration. This is the origin of the resin pockets so unpopular in timber processing.

Diagram 4

Characteristics of the ray system in broadleaved species. The schematic representation shows the characteristics in tangential and radial sections; differences in the cell arrangement permit classification into homogeneous and heterogeneous rays.

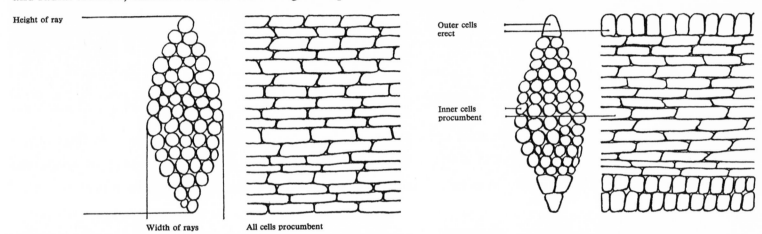

Height of ray

Width of rays

All cells procumbent

Outer cells erect

Inner cells procumbent

Homogeneous ray
Axes of outer and inner cells are parallel to the ray axis
Example: Acer

Heterogeneous ray
Axes of outer cells are perpendicular to the ray axis: inside, the cell axes and the ray axis are parallel
Example: Ilex

In a radial section all axial cells are cut longitudinally. The tracheids are revealed here as cells closed on both sides with a great many bordered pits in their radial longitudinal walls. These bordered pits are valves through which rising water can pass from cell to cell. Diagram 3 shows clearly that this valve action is effected by a torus located at the center of the pit membrane adhering, according to the prevailing water pressure, either to the left or to the right of the forked bulge of the secondary wall. The vessels in the wood of broadleaves require no such device because the individual vessel members have larger or smaller lumina and are either open or inadequately closed at their ends. Occasionally we find ladder-shaped (or scalariform) pitting, as for instance in Plate 66 f, g (birch). Plate 66 e, f further shows that fibers, like tracheids, are cells closed at both ends, although shorter and with narrower lumina. The rays are also cut along their principal axis in radial longitudinal section so that minute structural characteristics become visible. Among conifers, for instance, pines differ from firs in that their outer rows of rays consist of serrated ray tracheids (Plate 65 K) and the inner ones of parenchyma and occasionally resin canal tissue. In firs (Plate 65 H) the rays are comprised only of parenchyma. The rays in hardwood can be divided into homogeneous rays, in which all parenchyma cells are procumbent, and heterogeneous rays, with rectangular or square outer cells (Diagram 4) and procumbent inner cells. Viewed radially the rays occasionally reveal embedded crystals, as in ebony (Plate 66 q), or inclusions of heartwood substances as in beech (Plate 66 h).

Diagram 5

Pattern of ray arrangement. The two tangential sections show (on the left) an irregular arrangement of rays and (on the right) the rays arranged in storeys one above the other.

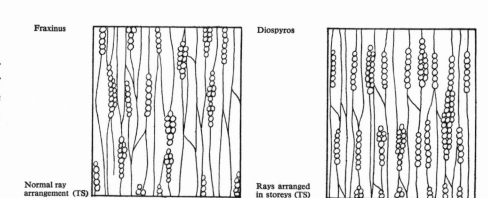

Fraxinus

Diospyros

Normal ray arrangement (TS)

Rays arranged in storeys (TS)

In a tangential section the rays are cut at right angles to their own longitudinal axis so that their structure and arrangement can be observed with particular clarity. In most kinds of wood rays are dispersed irregularly within the basic tissue, as in ash (Diagram 5; Plate 66 i). Other species show a layered structure, with the rays lying at different levels, as in ebony (Diagram 5; Plate 66 n). The rays vary considerably in tangential width: alongside uniseriate rays in Spanish chestnut or ebony (Plate 66 n) there are multiseriate ones, as in ash (Plate 66 i). In oak rays more than twenty cells wide can be observed (Plate 66 o) alongside small uniseriate ones. These massive rays have been formed by the fusion of small rays, in accordance with the pattern shown in Diagram 6. Very wide rays occur mainly in oak and beech. Hornbeam or alder may seem to possess broad rays when viewed by naked eye; under the microscope, however, it is found that these seemingly wide ray zones are made up of numerous narrow rays with interposed fibers (Diagram 7; Plate 66 p). Rays of this type are known as aggregate rays. Since fibers are sometimes discovered running through the wide rays in oak, aggregate rays may probably be seen as a stage in the development of true wide rays. It can be demonstrated that the rays have been variously modified in the course of the phylogenetic development of broadleaved trees. The formation of homogeneous from heterogeneous rays, for instance, is explained by the loss or reduction of wings on both sides of the heterogeneous rays (Diagram 8) and the formation of uniseriate rays by reduction of the multiseriate central part of heterogeneous rays. Incidentally, rays in softwood are arranged and structured far more uniformly than in the wood of broadleaves. In tangential section they reveal themselves as narrow uniseriate bands (Plate 65 E, F) with the exception of resinous woods in which some rays have fusiform widenings which enclose a transverse resin canal.

In tangential section, in much the same way as in a radial plane, the fibers, vessels and parenchyma strands are cut longitudinally. Among conifers, Douglas fir and yew show helical thickenings in longitudinal tracheids (Plate 65 F), while in the wood of broadleaves fibers with septa can occasionally be observed. These are incomplete intermediate membranes which, though extending from one longitudinal

Diagram 6

Evolution of multiseriate rays. The figures show rays cut in tangential direction.

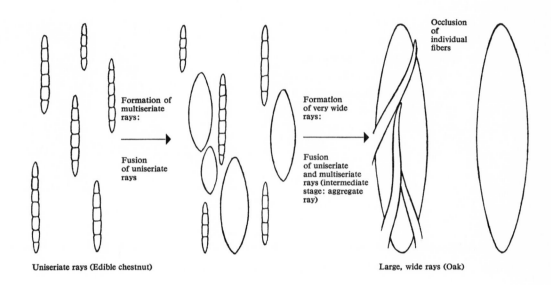

Uniseriate rays (Edible chestnut)

Formation of multiseriate rays:

Fusion of uniseriate rays

Formation of very wide rays:

Fusion of uniseriate and multiseriate rays (intermediate stage: aggregate ray)

Occlusion of individual fibers

Large, wide rays (Oak)

wall in the cell to another, nevertheless fail to achieve complete separation across the lumen. Septate wood fibers are known in many species of the Meliaceae family and also in Entandrophragma (Plate 66m). Plates 66i, k also show very clearly how the individual vessel members join up to form long vascular tubes. In their terminal zones such vascular tubes are in contact with others, so that a continuous vascular system exists in the stem. Much the same is true of the parenchyma strand cells which form a continuous system in the stem even though individual transverse sections may convey the impression of isolated cells.

Examination of the three principal sections through a stem makes it possible to pinpoint the location of various cells and to describe tissues and tissue complexes. Proportion, length and diameter of the principal cell types of some common tree species can be tabulated as follows:

Wood	Mean proportion of tracheids in %	Length of tracheids in mm	Diameter μ	Wood	Mean proportion of vessels in %	Length of vessel members μ	Diameter μ	Wood	Mean proportion of fibers	Fiber length in mm	Diameter μ
Spruce	95.3	1.7–3.7	20–40	Maple	6.9	300	30–110	Maple	75.9	0.7–1.1	10–20
Silver fir	90.4	3.4–4.6	25–65	Birch	24.7	300–600	30–130	Birch	64.8	0.8–1.6	14–40
Scotch pine	93.1	1.4–4.4	10–50	Beech	31.0	300–700	5–10	Beech	37.4	0.6–1.3	16–22
White pine	94.0	1.4–3.2	40–70	Oak	7.7	100–400	10–400	Oak	58.1	0.6–1.6	10–30
Larch	91.2	2.3–4.3	20–60	Ash	12.1	150–250	14–350	Ash	62.0	0.2–1.6	9–50
				Linden	17.0	400	20–90	Linden	72.0	0.5–1.4	10–30
				Walnut	12.0	100–600	60–240	Walnut	63.8	1.0–2.0	20
				Poplar	26.4	500	20–150	Poplar	59.0	0.7–1.6	29–44
				Elm	29.0	100–200	20–340	Elm	51.0	0.9–2.4	10–60

Diagram 7

Diagram of an aggregate ray. Whitebeam or alder, if viewed with the unaided eye, show wide ray zones; under the microscope, however, these are revealed as an accumulation of lesser rays embedded among the fibers.

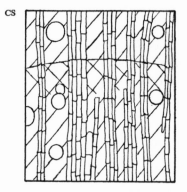

Carpinus   TS   CS

Aggregate rays (Carpinus and Alnus):
Zone with accumulation of lesser rays, separated from each other only by basic fiber tissue and not by vascular strands

Having acquainted ourselves with the morphology of softwood and hardwood tissue systems we now see that they perform exceedingly important physiological functions in the living tree. The early wood tracheids of conifers and the vessels of broadleaves permit the conduct of water while the late wood tracheids of conifers and the fibers of broadleaves ensure their mechanical strength; in both types the parenchyma strand and ray parenchyma cells allow storage. Living trees require enormous quantities of water, all of which is taken up by the roots and transferred through the stem to the crown for transpiration. In trees above a certain age, water conduction takes place only in the sapwood zone. This peripheral ring of active wood surrounds an inner core of wood which has been relieved of vital physiological functions. According to the arrangement of the water conduction system the water-conducting zone can be relatively wide (in conifers and diffuse-porous broadleaves) or narrow, sometimes embracing only a few growth rings (in ring-porous broadleaved species). The closure mechanism of internal water channels prevents the penetration of air into water-conducting tubes; in conifers this is achieved through adhesion of the pit tori to the outer pit borders and in broadleaves by the formation of tyloses. These are balloon-shaped inward bulges of ray or parenchyma strand cells into neighboring vessels (Plate 66h–beech) through common pit apertures. The cells serving rigidity are as a rule thick-walled and more or less extensively lignified (Plate 65 D). The cell walls in wood consist, apart from cellulose as a scaffold substance, of hemicellulose and lignin. Lignin is the wood substance proper and only appears in the phylogenetic development of the plant kingdom with the change from aquatic to terrestrial existence. Lignin forms a crust, thus hardening the cell wall and lending it the requisite rigidity. Conifers exposed to excessive loads, for instance through unilateral wind action or heavy snow pressure, develop cells with particularly massive walls. In this so-called compression wood the longitudinal cell walls are sheared and develop cracks (Plate 65 I), but they are thicker and more highly lignified than in normal wood. Hardwood reacts somewhat differently to excessive stress of this kind. It forms tension wood in which the cells again possess greatly thickened walls (Plate 66 l) but store more cellu-

Diagram 8

Evolution of heterogeneous into homogeneous or uniseriate rays. The diagram shows the rays cut in their tangential direction and elucidates the evolutionary modifications in the ray system.

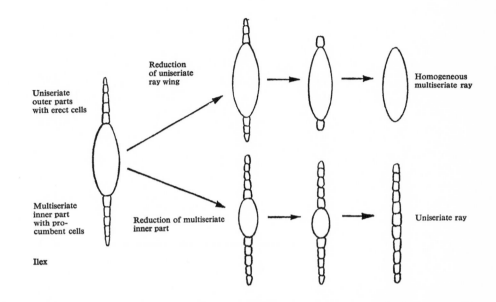

Uniseriate outer parts with erect cells

Reduction of uniseriate ray wing

Homogeneous multiseriate ray

Multiseriate inner part with procumbent cells

Reduction of multiseriate inner part

Uniseriate ray

Ilex

lose in the innermost, gelatinous, layer. The thickness of a cell wall, however, can vary greatly in accordance with the genetic factors of a species, regardless of external factors. Thus the cork tree (balsa) forms gossamer-thin cell walls whereas those of box wood are exceedingly thick and dense. Differences in cell wall thickness are observed within the same annual ring, due to the change from early to late wood (Plate 65 D). Another exceedingly important function is the storage of substances in parenchyma cells. By assimilating CO_2 the leaves and needles of massive tree crowns as a rule produce a surplus of sugar which is transferred through the descending phloem bundles to the lower parts of the stem and thence through rays radially into the stem. It is always sugar that is transferred, whereas starch is stored; the storage cells must possess a well-equipped fermentation system to enable this kind of conversion to take place. The storage cells in the sapwood are therefore alive and exceedingly active whereas the vessels and fibers are dead and perform their function only as empty chambers. Living cells can be recognized by their protoplasmic content, above all by their cell nucleus and plasma (Plate 65 K). As a rule they are still filled with grains of starch and with fatty substances. With the conversion of sapwood into heartwood these reserves are transferred and simultaneously the living cells lose their vitality: they undergo necrobiosis. The formation of heartwood, seen in this light, may be characterized as normal physiological aging of wood tissue. Heartwood formation is frequently accompanied by inner stem zone pigmentation, resulting in a hardwood formation. Pigment may be kept back in the storage system in certain species, as in ash or beech (Plate 66 h), while in others, as in oak or pine, it is embedded in the cell walls. Such differences produce variations in the technological parameters just as much as do differences in wood morphology.

An astonishing variety is displayed in the structure and growth of wood. On the microscopic and sub-microscopic scale wood reveals an unsuspected beauty which fascinates the observer and makes him begin to understand why it forms part of the history of mankind.

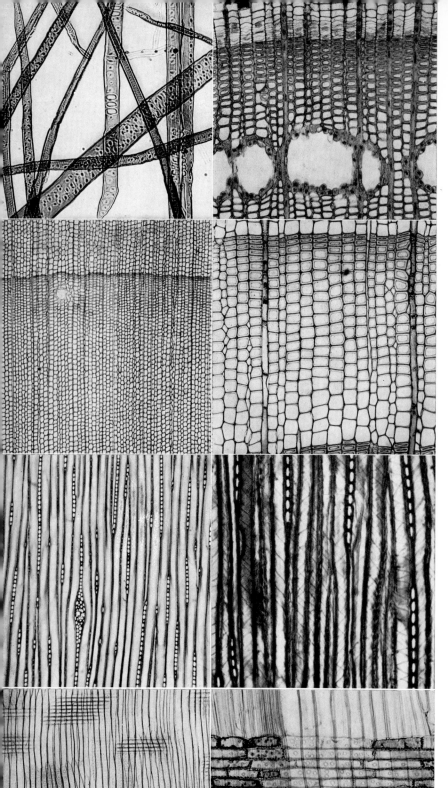

A	B
C	D
E	F
G	H
I	K

a	b	c	d
e	f	g	h
i	k	l	m
n	o	p	q
r	s	t	u

65 Softwoods

A   Individual cells of softwood; 80:1

B   *Scotch pine*, cross-section, cambium, on the outside phloem, on the inside xylem; 40:1

C   *Scotch pine*, cross-section, basic tissue of longitudinal tracheids and axial resin canal; 30:1

D   *Silver fir*, cross-section, early wood with narrow and late wood with wide cell membranes; 110:1

E   *Larch*, tangential section, longitudinal tracheids and rays; 55:1

F   *Yew*, tangential section, longitudinal tracheids with spiral thickenings; 170:1

G   *Stone pine*, radial section, basic tracheid tissue and rays; 50:1

H   *Silver fir*, radial section, medullar ray composed only of parenchyma cells, growth ring boundary; 125:1

I   *Scotch pine*, radial section, stressed wood with shear fissures in the tracheids; 200:1

K   *Scotch pine*, radial section, ray with ray tracheids (serrated) and parenchyma cell (nucleus and plasma); 600:1

66 Hardwoods

a   Individual cells of hardwood; 80:1

b   *Oak*, cross-section, ring-porous arrangement of vessels; 80:1

c   *Poplar*, cross-section, diffuse-porous arrangement of vessels; 80:1

d   *Cherry*, cross-section, semi-ring-porous arrangement of vessels; 40:1

e   *Oak*, radial section; 30:1

f   *Birch*, radial section, vessels with scalariform perforations; 150:1

g   *Birch*, radial section, scalariform perforations of vessels; 670:1

h   *Beech*, radial section, vessels blocked by tyloses and storage tissue with occlusions of pigment nuclei; 65:1

i   *Ash*, tangential section, conducting vessels and fibers axial, rays across; 70:1

k   *Oak*, tangential section, water-conducting vessels composed of individual vessel links; 115:1

l   *Beech*, cross-section, tension wood: fibers with thick-walled gelatinous layer; 500:1

m   *Entandrophragma*, tangential section, septated fiber; 320:1

n   *Ebony*, tangential section, stratification of rays; 50:1

o   *Oak*, tangential section, very wide ray with fiber occlusions; 40:1

p   *Alder*, cross-section, aggregate ray; 30:1

q   *Ebony*, radial section, ray cells with crystals; 115:1

r   *Oak*, cross-section, apotracheal diffuse parenchyma; 50:1

s   *Ebony*, cross-section, vasicentric parenchyma; 115:1

t   *Pterocarpus*, cross-section, aliform parenchyma; 125:1

u   *Shorea*, cross-section, banded parenchyma; 55:1

67 Dead ivy on a tree bark with lichen

68 Ivy *(Hedera helix)*, climbing up a tree trunk

Forestry and Wood Processing

Carl Lanz

Like everything else on earth, the forest in all its variety is subject to the inexorable laws of nature. As a complex living association of plants and animals, it is continually changing, always pursuing the ultimate goal of all living things–self-preservation. Each member is engaged in a ceaseless struggle for existence, a struggle in which the stronger is the ultimate winner.

This natural selection has been quietly taking place in the primeval forest over thousands of years, and it explains why the forests of the Far North and along the upper tree line are composed of only a few frost-resisting conifers capable of standing up to the harsh climate. With increasing warmth and longer vegetation periods, these are joined by other and more demanding broadleaved trees and shrubs until we end up in the almost impenetrable tropical forest with its exceedingly large number of species. These ecological associations are in a biological balance, invariably striving to preserve themselves and adapt themselves to environmental conditions through further selection.

A prerequisite of any systematic forest management is a forest survey to determine surface and wood resources. Another important aspect is the composition of the growing stock in terms of species and the rate of its increase. It is the task of forestry management to ascertain these production elements and all other factors of importance to wood production. Forest areas of major extent are nowadays chiefly recorded by aerial photography. The pictures so obtained make it possible, in conjunction with photographs taken on the ground, to apply statistical methods for the determination of wood resources and their composition. These modern methods of inventory taking are increasingly applied also to lesser forest areas whose wood resources have hitherto been computed by the time-consuming measurement of individual trees or by other conventional methods. It is important to ascertain wood resources accurately because they represent the product appropriate to the given soil and climate. Wood grows only on wood; the trees in a given forest, therefore, are simultaneously the means of production and the product. This dual function distinguishes the forest from industrial production. If it is to continue supplying timber it cannot simply be extracted like a raw material deposit which does not renew itself, but must instead be preserved as an entity.

There are various methods of ascertaining timber growth; one such method is the comparison of two calculations of standing timber made at different times, with allowance being made for the timber withdrawn, and the withdrawal of core samples from growing or from felled trees. The data thus obtained allow reliable conclusions to be drawn as to growth and volume. Stocks of standing timber, its composition and growth rate are the most important data for long-term management. They determine the allowable cut–the quantity of timber which may be felled within a given period according to forestry-management considerations. (As a general principle no more wood should be withdrawn from a forest than is renewed in it.) These data are laid down in an economic management plan which moreover contains information on all forestry or lumbering procedures for the most economic production of timber: the opening up of a forest, construction of tracks, cableways or water supplies in accordance with anticipated timber production.

Management therefore occupies an important position in forestry. It must not only ascertain existing stocks but possess information on how much can be produced and used and where and over what period of time. To meet this task it must base itself on the findings of numerous other branches of forestry, in particular on silviculture which defines the natural possibilities of increasing timber production in line with the chosen economic target in terms of species, methods of renewal, stand patterns and management. The complex problems associated with this will be discussed elsewhere in this book.

Wood production and forest utilization

The mere existence of forests in which wood grows is not in itself enough to meet requirements. The wood must first be cut, prepared, hauled out of the forest and processed. Cutting and hauling the logs to the loading points is a difficult enterprise, demanding specialized skills and, where modern equipment is used, technical competence. Only a few decades ago it was still customary, even in highly developed industrial countries, to fell even the biggest trees with axe and handsaw; nowadays power saws are employed even in the remotest parts of the forest. The timber is mechanically loaded on to the trucks and in the shortest possible time taken to the nearest mill or railroad. A certain romance has thereby vanished from our forests.

In the primeval forest the employment of technical aids is nowadays indispensable to an economic production of timber. Bulldozers slice through the thickest tropical vegetation which is virtually impenetrable to man. Tracked vehicles haul the massive logs along hazardous roads to distant transhipment ports. Only occasionally is tropical timber processed into boards or beams in primitive mills in the immediate neighborhood; most of the time the necessary technical equipment is lacking. In the tropics, as in other remote regions, machines have largely replaced manual work. But the wear and tear on them is considerable, owing to the exceptional demands made by the climate, the nature and dimensions of the timber, and the lack of expert maintenance. Thus, in spite of frequently modest wages, production and transport costs are high.

The importance attached to improvements in timber production is revealed in Canada and the United States, in Scandinavia and even in Russia, where in government or privately managed institutes hundreds and even thousands of engineers, technicians and specialists are engaged in the construction of machines, the development of cost-effective working methods and the testing of practical innovations. In the wooded regions of these countries we encounter track-laying vehicles which, by means of frontally mounted circular saws or powerful shears cut the trees, load them and carry them to fully mechanized processing centers. There they are trimmed of their branches, stripped of their bark, cut into definite lengths and, sorted according to diameter, loaded onto the rail cars–all by remote control. The entire operation from the stump to the sawmill or into the chemical plant takes place without a single worker making contact with the tree. This use of machinery increases the productivity of labor by ten or more times compared with traditional methods. However, these processes can be applied only in extensive, relatively open and usually homogeneous forests such as those in the northern plains, where neither protective nor recreational aspects need be taken into account, and where the climate and the soil make it possible, without appreciable damage in the future, to clear-cut the stands over a large area and either to reforest them or leave their slow restocking to nature. Only a short distance further south, where precipitation no longer falls mainly as snow, where an almost impermeable soil causes water-logging or swamp formation, or where denuded hillsides lead to erosion, this kind of wood production would result in grave damage. The warmer the climate and the steeper the ground, the more must wood production be restricted to relatively small areas, down to individual tree utilization, to make sure the vulnerable forest soil remains protected from direct sunlight and lashing rain and preserves the fertility it has achieved through being sheltered under a continuous canopy. The fully mechanized enterprises with their giant machines in the Far North and in the west of the United States, however, account only for a small portion of the world's total wood production. Generally speaking, manual work still predominates, although the power saw penetrates deeper and deeper into the dense tropical forest and into remote mountain forests in the train of technical progress.

Logging and hauling to the main traffic routes are calculated to require between two and three working hours per cubic meter of wood. Wood production and hauling in the forest therefore require an annual expenditure of roughly 15,000 million working hours a year and approximately as many dollars, the major part for the payment of wages. Because of the considerable proportion of cheap fuelwood and because of the low financial yield even of commercial timber in technically unfavorably situated forests, the value of the wood itself comes to rather less than the production costs. On a rough average it amounts, at most, to half the harvesting costs or about 5,000 to 7,000 million dollars. Thus a good two-thirds of the market price is due to the harvesting and hauling of the undressed timber. Considering the marked rise in wages throughout the world in recent years, forestry managers in all countries see themselves faced by the compelling need to reduce the wage element of their expenditure as far as possible through mechanization, to enable wood to compete successfully with other construction and working materials. The large labor force needed also explains the massive technical and organizational efforts of timber producing countries to achieve the industrial methods of production we have described.

When timber is ready for processing it leaves the immediate sphere of forestry. The various types of undressed timber are channeled to consumers directly or through the trade and are processed according to intended use by hand, machine or chemical.

Commercial wood and fuelwood

About half the total wood harvest nowadays is accounted for by commercial wood of all kinds; the rest is fuelwood. The importance of the latter has been steadily declining since the emergence of such power sources as coal, electricity and oil, and more recently, nuclear power. In highly industrialized countries, such as the U.S.A., Canada and Russia, as well as in Britain and Germany, the share of fuelwood amounts to a mere 10 to 20 per cent, while in the less developed countries it predominates with 70 to 90 per cent.

Fuelwood undergoes the least transformation before consumption. Frequently collected straight from the forest, it is cut up by axe or handsaw. The rural housewife then uses it as firewood over which she cooks meals for the family and fodder for the livestock. During the cold season an open fire will flicker in the kitchen or a venerable old stove will warm a sparsely lit parlor–to many people a picture from great-grandfather's days. And yet millions of people are to this day dependent on fuelwood, that stepchild of the technological age. They will roam under a scorching sun for hours on end in order to collect a small bundle of thin sticks from the infrequent shrubs of treeless steppes. Abundance on one side, an acute shortage on the other–this is still frequently the unequal pattern of fuelwood supplies. Because of its low heating value per volume and weight it does not justify long-distance transportation. If it has to be transported over a great distance its price rises beyond the reach of the poor. Thus a daily ration of 6 lbs. of fuelwood, sufficient for cooking a single meal for a family of five in one of the major towns in the steppe area south of the Sahara cost about 40 cents in 1962–more than one-third of the daily earnings of a native worker at that time. Small wonder that in spite of all prohibitions those people used every opportunity to break off a branch or two from the few trees found in the neighborhood in order to smuggle them into their poor hovels in the dark of a tropical night. Trade in fuelwood there is subject to a permit and the approaches to the towns are strictly guarded during the day. It is obvious that under these circumstances it is difficult to carry out the reforestation decreed by the government to combat the wood shortage. As a rule young trees are cut down by the population before they have even grown to the thickness of a human arm. Not only fuelwood but also posts and poles are much in demand in those regions and fetch a high price of roughly 30 cents per linear yard or $1.50 per cubic foot. Yet six or seven years would be enough for fast-growing teak or eucalyptus trees to produce the material urgently needed for building simple huts.

Conditions are entirely different in the more heavily wooded countries, where such wood is left lying in the forests because no one wants it even free of charge. And yet the young stands must be thinned out if they are to produce valuable commercial timber in the future. Attempts are now being made in various European countries to machine-process the traditional forest trimmings, which are no longer in demand as fuel, in order to utilize them in modern fully-automatic boiler plants merely to cover costs, or to process them into particle boards and cellulose.

Charcoal burning is nowadays practised only in remote and less developed regions. Once large quantities of wood were turned into charcoal, originally in piles and later in retorts, and carried over often considerable distances for domestic, commercial or industrial use. Iron foundries and glassworks, in particular, required enormous quantities, and this led to the denuding of entire valleys. Until the turn of the century, tar and acetic acid were valuable by-products of the retort process, though today these are obtained far more cheaply, and in chemically purer form, by way of synthesis or through the coking of coal. Charcoal production, therefore, apart from a few strictly limited areas, is of scarcely any economic significance nowadays. Even the active charcoal which is of military importance for the filters of gasmasks is now more advantageously produced from coal.

When European countries were suffering a shortage of gasoline and diesel fuel during World War II, charcoal, and wood itself, once more came into their own as substitute fuels. Thousands of otherwise useless automobiles, tractors and stationary installations were equipped with generators and fueled with wood or charcoal; in this way essential field work and transportation were made possible. Even the warring armies derived valuable services from these solid fuels. The generator method has since been further developed. It is now possible to convert engines from diesel fuel to wood gas at a moment's notice and without appreciable loss of performance. Wood gas makes it possible to save 70 to 80 per cent of diesel fuel–a potentially important figure in times of shortage.

Because fuelwood is increasingly squeezed out by cheaper and, above all, more convenient sources of energy, firing installations are being steadily improved. Alongside wood-dust furnaces for large plants there are modern wood cookers and heating plants in numerous countries, sometimes combined with electricity or oil. These compare well with other heat sources in terms of cleanliness and convenience. Provided the user has at his disposal storage facilities and his own wood supply, as is usually the case in rural areas, such installations are considerably cheaper than any form of power that has to be purchased. Yet even the most up-to-date furnaces are unlikely to halt the decline in the use of fuelwood in countries with a high standard of living. But they do help to slow down the trend and to gain time for the discovery of new uses. These, as far as one can tell today, lie in industrial utilization of wood for panels, cellulose and paper, consumption of which is continuously rising throughout the world. It is undoubtedly only a question of time before this source of raw material latent in fuelwood is utilized to an even greater extent.

Whereas in the industrialized countries of the temperate zone forestry managements are trying to find buyers for fuelwood, in arid treeless regions, as has been shown by the African example, their task consists in remedying the shortage of fuelwood through forestation. In spite of the decline in the consumption of fuelwood in industrialized countries, world-wide requirements are expected to increase over the next ten to twenty years because of the marked population increase and the progressive rise in the standard of living of developing regions. This is the conclusion of detailed studies by the Food and Agriculture Organization (F.A.O.) which, on the basis of assessments in various countries, expect a roughly 40 per cent increase in consumption by 1975. This means a requirement of 42,400 million cubic feet (1,200 million cubic meters) of fuelwood compared with 31,800 million cubic feet (900 million cubic meters) at the beginning of the sixties.

Far more important economically than fuelwood is the wood processed industrially into a great variety of products. The list is headed by roundwood as the raw material for boards and beams. In 1967 world production of sawn timber amounted to over 13,000 million cubic feet. This required roughly 17,000 million cubic feet of coniferous and 5,300 million cubic feet of broadleaved wood, totalling 22,300 million cubic feet.

Modern processing of wood

Boards and beams are still the best known wood products. Thousands of years ago heavy round logs were first rough-hewn with axes into squared off planks and building timbers for the construction of bridges, simple dwellings and elaborate temples, furniture and vehicles. The saw, too, is an ancient tool, used with great skill by the Egyptians who sawed the choicest timbers into wafer-thin sheets called veneers for the decoration of coffers and cabinets. In remote regions, where roads or rivers for transportation are lacking but where sufficient human labour is available, boards and beams are to this day laboriously worked by hand with axe or saw, to make the timber suitable for transport to villages and cities by cart, beast of burden or files of porters.

A modern sawmill presents a very different picture. Here the logs arrive by the thousands, brought by truck, rail or ship, or floated down rivers either singly or in rafts. Powerful cranes with specially shaped grabs unload the vehicles, sort the timber and stack it. From the stack or from the log pond, log after log, untouched by human hand, is carried by conveyors and rollers towards highly efficient saws. Their sharp teeth bite into the log, slicing it longitudinally, with an accuracy of a small fraction of an inch. The log thus leaves the saws as a number of separate boards. Through sophisticated, electronically controlled sorting devices and through further woodworking machines the sawn wood eventually reaches the drying chambers in batches or is stacked in the open. Like the biggest timber-producing enterprises, these industrialized sawmills are found in America, Scandinavia and Russia. In other countries there is still a predominance of small mills with a marked artisan character. Scattered throughout the country, they are located as close as possible to their source of raw material, the forest.

Sawn wood is subsequently processed into crates, building timber or furniture or else supplied to carpenters' or joiners' shops and to other consumers. Considerable quantities of sawn wood are exported, mostly by ship, from the great timber surplus areas to the commercial and consumer centers of the industrialized countries.

By far the most important consumers of sawn wood everywhere are the building industry and its associated wood-processing trades; they account for between two-thirds and four-fifths of the total production. Boards and beams are needed for virtually every building operation, either as an auxiliary material for shuttering and scaffolding or as the building material proper for walls, ceilings and roof structures. This is the realm of the carpenter who, perched high up in the air, joins the separate joists into rounded domes, slender spires pointing to the sky, or simple ridged roofs; in many countries the completion of his work is marked by the topping-out ceremony. Inside, wood is used in a great variety of ways. Plain or elaborately curved staircases link one floor with another. The joiner installs windows, doors and panelings or fits built-in wall cupboards. Finally, the house is comfortably equipped with furniture and other objects of daily use. Even in the most modern buildings, constructed by the latest methods in steel or concrete, wood is invariably found in some form or other. Indeed, modern man experiences a need for rest and shelter and tries to relax from his enervating activity within his domestic environment. There is perhaps no other material which can give him this comforting atmosphere more than wood with its close-ness to nature.

The second most important use for sawn wood is in crates and other forms of packaging. These products account for about 15 to 20 per cent of the world's total consumption of sawn wood. We need only think of the massive crates in which machines weighing many tons are packaged, waterproofed and protected from mechanical damage, and transported over thousands of miles. The engineering industry, whenever it builds some large plant for export, is one of the most important consumers of sawn wood. Wines and spirits used to be stored in wooden barrels before reaching the consumer. The most recently developed common wood product is the pallet on which small items are economically transported and stored.

Until about a hundred years ago wood was indispensable in shipbuilding. Merchant fleets and, more espe-cially, navies consumed enormous quantities of high-quality timber, mainly durable oakwood and resin-ous coniferous wood. The heavy demand led to the denudation of vast regions, such as the Lebanese for-ests by the Phoenicians and the karst in Yugoslavia by the Venetians. To ensure wood supplies forests were laid out or existing forests managed with an eye to the production of shipbuilding timber. The oak stands seen today in Stockholm were, at the time, planted for this purpose. Military requirements, for in-stance, the supply of wheelwright timber for gun carriages and supply wagons, led to the planting of ave-nues of trees; near Berne for example the exit roads are lined with massive elms. Since the industrial manu-facture of iron and steel, timber has lost its former great importance in this field. Nowadays it is virtually used only for the construction of small boats or for specialized vessels like minesweepers, or, in vehicle construction, for floors and wall panels.

Railways need cross-ties to carry the rails. Alongside steel and, more recently, concrete, these ties are of predominantly broadleaved or coniferous wood. The world's rail network amounts to nearly 870,000 miles for which approximately 2,000 million wooden cross-ties have been used. To extend their useful life they are usually impregnated with preservatives. Even so they have to be replaced every fifteen to twenty years, according to the kind of wood, climate and extent of use, and this means an annual requirement of about 120 million cross-ties or roughly 880 million cubic feet of logs. The railroad cross-tie is one of the few wood products which, in remote regions to this day, is worked by axe in the forest.

High-quality logs of common woods and all logs of rare choice woods are usually peeled with large knives. In this way thin wood foils known as veneers are produced. Compared with sawing this method has the advantage of less waste, which means a more economical use of particularly precious woods. The veneers, which are frequently less than one millimeter (one twenty-fifth of an inch) thick, are glued together either crosswise with one another to make plywood or on a solid base to produce large sheets particularly suitable for further processing. These methods, too, were known to the ancient Egyptians, as is attested by the discovery of three-ply sheets of wood and of veneered parts of tomb furniture. Another form of wood sheet is blockboard, which consists of a central layer of small jointed wood battens between two layers of veneer. All these sheets used to be produced by craftsmen. This made them expensive and confined their use to luxury furniture. Only when it became possible, about the turn of the century, to manufacture wood panels industrially in large quantities and hence at a lower price, did they come into common use. Since the 1930's in particular, plywood has been used for a great variety of purposes, whenever stability, a high degree of rigidity and lightness are important–in vehicle construction, in containers, and above all in furniture making and internal fittings; these today are its main applications. The raw material for facing veneers, for covering the visible surfaces of furniture and wall panelings, are colored and usually hard choice woods such as walnut, oak and maple, but can also be precious exotic woods including species of mahogany, teak and palisander. The inner plies in plywood or blockboard, as well as the hidden veneers to balance the precious top layers, are made from cheaper, usually blond and soft woods such as poplar, obeche and okumé. In North America, coniferous woods are largely used. The total world production of the still relatively young veneer and plywood industry in 1967 was over 880 million cubic feet of plywood and veneers, requiring nearly 1,800 million cubic feet of good to top-quality logs.

Industrial timber

Another important type is industrial timber. This term covers small logs of about 3 to 10 inch diameter which, on the one hand, are not suitable for processing into sawn wood or veneers but, on the other, are of higher quality than fuelwood. Industrial timber is sold in bulk; it is the principal raw material for cellulose, paper board and paper, as well as for fiberboard and particle board, and in smaller quantities also for wood wool. Though relatively young, these industries have developed at an extraordinary pace and their timber requirements have been steadily increasing. In 1967 world consumption of industrial timber was roughly 12,700 million cubic feet for paper products and about 1,060 million cubic feet for panels. Unlike log wood, the raw material for the fiber and particle board industry is finely shredded, and often indeed chemically dissolved, for the manufacture of large-dimension homogeneous products from the various constituents. Wet pulping of round timbers usually about 3 feet long produces wood pulp, the main constituent of newsprint and paperboard. For cellulose manufacture the wood is finely shredded and boiled with water and chemicals at a high temperature to dissolve the lignin, the second component of wood, as well as other occluded substances. Filters and heated rollers remove the surplus water from the cellulose pulp. The dried cellulose is taken to the paper mills, where it is mixed with wood pulp and additives according to the desired quality of the finished product.

According to the process used we distinguish three types of cellulose–sulfate, sulfite and hemi-cellulose (or half-stuff). The first of these processes is of particular interest to forestry because it can use a great many wood species which are less suitable for pulping or for the sulfite method. Hemi-cellulose only partially consists of cellulose, its other part consisting of incompletely broken-down wood fibers. It is the youngest member in the series of paper raw materials and, compared with pure cellulose, has the advantage of better utilization of the wood. Whereas for pure cellulose the yield related to the wood substance amounts to 40 to 50 per cent, it reaches 70 per cent and more for hemi-cellulose. The highest fiber yield is achieved by wood pulp with over 80 per cent. High-quality paper consists almost exclusively of cellulose. For ordinary paper and for wrapping paper, unbleached sulfite or sulfate cellulose is used as a rule, whereas newsprint and paperboard contain a large amount of wood pulp. Hemi-cellulose is added in smaller quantities than pure cellulose to the paper mass, and is above all used for corrugated cardboard. The semi-chemical method makes it possible to process various wood species jointly–a fact which is of special advantage in areas with broadleaved forests containing a large number of species (in contrast to the boreal coniferous belt which extends from Alaska across Labrador, Scandinavia and Karelia deep into Siberia). From the lignin-containing sulfite liquor may be obtained useful by-products such as alcohol and yeast; additionally, valuable chemicals are extracted. Wood can also be broken down into sugar. But sugar production from wood is not economical under normal market conditions because the sugar obtained can be produced more cheaply from other raw materials. Chemical processing of timber makes it possible to utilize up to 90 per cent of the wood substance.

Among the most recent industrial wood products are fiberboard and particle board. Fiberboard is a paper industry product and consists of matted wood fibers. When lightly compressed and porous, it represents an excellent insulating material against temperature fluctuations and sound; highly compressed it is a construction material similar to plywood and, with plastic laminate bonded on, produces decorative hard-wearing sheets for furniture and interior fittings. Particle board was developed in Europe during World War II and has only been mass produced since 1950. It soon spread rapidly in most industrial countries and has lately been manufactured in developing countries. Undressed wood is chopped into small chippings or planed into thin shavings. The loose wood particles are dried in special large-scale installations, glued in the airstream and poured into a paste-like mass which is subsequently passed through heated presses. Glazing rollers then smooth the surface of the compact sheets, longitudinal and cross saws cut them down to the desired dimensions, and after a short conditioning this most modern wood product is ready for further use in construction.

Technology has thus succeeded in transforming seemingly worthless fuelwood or waste wood into a valuable material which combines in itself the advantages of solid wood–lightness, good insulation and, according to density, high rigidity–while at the same time largely eliminating its disadvantages, especially troublesome shrinking and warping. Small wonder that hardboard and particle board are enjoying great popularity and are on the way to replacing solid board and even blockboard in furniture manufacture and internal fittings. Almost any wood species is a suitable raw material for particle board, with the exception of those containing large quantities of tannin, like oak and chestnut. No great demands are made on the outward shape of the original material. Rather higher demands are made in the case of fiberboard since here, as with paper, the length of the fibers plays a vital part. Both board industries have become exceedingly welcome customers for forestry. At present they consume approximately 1,060 million cubic feet of rough timber and sawmill waste for the manufacture of roughly 13 million tons of board. Though still undergoing extensive technical development, the particle board industry has experienced an unprecedented upsurge as no other branch of wood processing.

Pit props are another form of industrial timber; previously required in large quantities in mining, demand has lately been declining both because less coal is being mined and because steel supports are being increasingly used. World consumption of pit props at present amounts to roughly 1,060 million cubic feet. Mention should finally be made of posts and poles. These include poles for overhead telephone wires and electricity supplies, scaffolding and building poles, as well as timber for fencing and barriers. The greatest demand for these is among the rural population but this demand is met from local forests. Actual consumption is therefore difficult to ascertain. The quantities involved are estimated to amount to roughly 3,500 million cubic feet or roughly 10 per cent of world supplies of commercial timber.

Wood products and the timber trade

The most important types of timber and the principal wood products manufactured from them have been listed above, but the possible uses of wood are infinite. No account of forestry and the timber economy would be complete without a mention of the timber trade. This trade represents the middleman between producers at each stage and the countless consumers. Its knowledge of the market and its frequently world-wide connections enable the trade to discover any wood species required and channel it to the processors in appropriate quantity and quality. Frequently raw materials and consumer are at a great distance from one another, as for instance in the case of tropical timbers of which only a small portion is processed in the country of origin and the larger part in other continents, or in the case of wood for the paper industry which is shipped from America and Russia as far as Japan or Central Europe. Vast quantities are shipped to the consumer areas every year, both by land and water. In 1967, for instance, the total world exports of logs amounted to 1,130 million cubic feet. Of this somewhat more than half was supplied by the tropics. Nearly 530 million cubic feet of timber for the paper industry was supplied to industrialized countries. The biggest proportion of foreign trade in wood products goes to sawn wood with nearly 1,800 million cubic feet. By comparison the world trade in artificial boards and veneers looks rather modest with a mere 140 million cubic feet. Of considerable importance is the international trade in cellulose and paper products. In 1967 countries with a surplus, especially Canada and Scandinavia, exported roughly 33 million tons to the consumer areas of the U.S.A., Central Europe and Japan. World trade in wood and wood products has been showing a marked increase over the past few years as the industrialized countries are less and less able to meet their rising demands from domestic production.

More impressive than the quantities is the value of exported forestry products. Thus in 1967 unprocessed timber amounted to 1,195 million dollars, sawn wood (including veneers and artificial boards) to 2,707 million dollars, and paper and paperboard to the astonishing sum of 4,833 million dollars–altogether therefore 8,700 million dollars or 5 per cent of the total world trade.

Heading the world trade list in forestry products (both import and export) were the countries of Europe with nearly 8,900 million dollars, followed by North America with 5,200 million. The remaining 4,500 million were shared among Asia with 2,300 million and the other continents and Russia. The economic importance of the world-wide timber trade and the extent to which it has developed in recent years are revealed by the following figures, taken, like the data above, from a recent F.A.O. publication:

Value of forestry products in billions of dollars

	1950	1960	1965	1969	1970
Sawn wood	10.3	12.9	15.5	18.0	18.6
Veneers and particle boards	1.0	3.0	4.7	6.6	7.2
Paper and paperboard	8.7	13.2	16.9	22.0	23.7
Other products	3.9	5.8	7.4	8.7	8.8
Total	23.9	34.9	44.5	55.3	58.3

The value of all semi-finished and finished products has increased. In the case of veneers and manufactured boards it has risen five-fold in less than twenty years. The value of paper products has doubled. Production of sawn wood has gone up by only 50 per cent while the increase in the value of other wood products has been even more modest, amounting to only one-third. It is an obvious fact and an unmistakable trend of future development that by far the greatest increase is in industrial products manufactured in highly mechanized and partially automated large-scale plants while the wood products of small enterprises, and of craftsmen's workshops, are increasingly eclipsed. This is particularly clear in the case of sawn wood, which until 1960 headed the list in terms of value but a mere five years later was far outstripped by paper products. The most recent studies suggest that this trend will, if anything, intensify so that wood will increasingly become an industrial raw material proper. Careful production and consumption analyses have led the Forestry Department of the F.A.O. to conclude that world-wide demand of timber in 1975 will be about half as great again as at the beginning of this decade, i.e. that it will amount to roughly 53,000 million cubic feet of commercial timber. The main causes of this unexpectedly steep rise in demand, according to the F.A.O. are the population increase and a higher per capita consumption stemming from an improved standard of living. At present, per capita consumption of commercial timber, on a world average, is roughly 5.3 cubic feet but it is considerably higher in industrialized than in technically backward countries. It is expected that most of the increased demand will be met from the forests of the temperate zone, principally by North America, because these countries are economically and technologically in a better position than the numerous developing countries for mobilizing their vast still untapped timber resources.

As for the separate categories of commercial timber, it is calculated that consumption of sawn wood will increase by about a quarter by the mid-seventies, to reach about 15,000 million cubic feet. The demand for manufactured board is expected to more than double, with a five-fold increase being predicted for particle board. Consumption of paper products in 1975 is estimate by the F.A.O. at about double the 1961 figure. The demand for packaging paper and paperboard will increase more steeply than for writing and printing paper. In view of these higher demands it may be expected that international trade in wood products will similarly increase its turnover, especially as it will have to meet the growing supply shortage of the industrialized countries by increased imports from surplus areas. The F.A.O. believes that consumer countries must import principally coniferous sawn wood, quality hardwoods and fiberwood. There should be no difficulty in obtaining sawn wood considering the favorable production potential of the northern regions. Supplies of broadleaved logs will probably be more difficult. The question widely asked is whether the developing countries will succeed in making available the quantities of timber required, seeing that accessible tropical forests have hitherto been ruthlessly exploited and that financial resources are as a rule lacking for penetration into remote regions. The greatest increase in demand will no doubt be for industrial timber, above all for fiber products. But this small-bulk raw material can be produced in a relatively short time. The F. A. O. therefore assumes that a substantial part of the expected consumption increase can be met by the planting of fast-growing species and better utilization of existing woodlands in the consumer countries themselves. The remainder should be obtainable, without great difficulties, by increased imports from the traditional surplus regions of the north.

75 African woodcutters with hand-saw
76 Floating of logs in the Congo
77 Timber trans-shipment point in an African estuary

78 Working elephant at a timber stack in Thailand

79 Timber transportation near Heinola, Finland

80 Timber being transported by the current of the Gâtineau River, Canada

81 Rafting channel in a torrent (Finland) ▷

82 Port Alberni, Vancouver Island, Canada ▷▷

83 Lumbering in Western Canada (Port Alberni, Vancouver)

84 Modern skilled lumberjacks felling a massive tree with power saws

85 Trunk of spruce *(Picea abies)* attacked by heartrot

89 Young stems being stripped of their bark with a draw-knife 90 Colorado Indian in Ecuador stripping off bark and working a stem into building planks for his hut

91 Brazilian natives building a wooden craft ▷

Welfare Functions of the Forest

Ernst Krebs

A forest does not merely consist of trees. Many trees do not make a forest, any more than many people make a nation. A nation is a community formed by the inhabitants of a country who are linked together by countless economic, cultural and ethical relationships, possessing a common tradition and rooted in a common soil. Similarly each forest is a unique complex community of ecologically related plants at tree, shrub and herbaceous levels, of the great multiplicity of wildlife belonging to it, of the flora and fauna of its soil. The vegetation cover of the forest with its densely interwoven roots is closely linked with the forest soil and forms with it an inseparable unity. The whole space from the highest treetops to the minutest ramifications of the roots teems with life of a great many kinds; everything that lives in this complex world of plants and animals is part of the forest, part of its entirety. This community is governed by biological laws decreed by nature. It comprises struggle but also mutual aid, expulsion and support, enmity and friendship; in it constructive and destructive forces interact. The tree itself is a miracle–that elaborate organism capable of pumping water from the soil into the air, taking on carbon dioxide from the air, producing carbohydrates like a chemical factory to feed men and beasts, enriching the air with oxygen, repeating nature's eternal cycle through hundreds of years. Yet in the green confusion of the forest the tree is just one creature among millions. The forest community thus mirrors the evolution of man and nations.

The effects of destruction

It is not difficult to upset the balance of this forest association. Anyone understanding the peculiarities of this harmonious and continuous association will realize the complex relationships which are cruelly disturbed by clear-cutting or tree clearance. He will also understand that a destroyed forest cannot simply be replaced by reforestation elsewhere. A newly planted forest is sociologically and ecologically not the same thing as an original forest, and for a protracted period it will not produce the same economic or shelter effect. An uninhabited tract of country can be resettled with people, but generations will come and go before these people form a real living nation. It takes a great deal of time before a forestation on formerly open land becomes a true forest with its natural structure; the ecological relationships of a living community form only gradually, as do the peculiar architecture of naturally-grown soil and the close link between vegetation cover and soil. Any interference with a region's existing forests therefore has far more weighty consequences than one might think at first, and the resulting destruction cannot be made good over a very long period in spite of the most generous reforestation.

Nor is it difficult to destroy a forest totally. Man has long been doing just this in the most blatant way through greed and a total claim on nature. The ancient civilized countries of the Mediterranean area were almost completely denuded of forests at an early date. In Asia gigantic forest areas were destroyed throughout a period of 1,000 to 2,000 years by overpopulation. Seemingly immeasurable forest expanses in the eastern United States, in the Mississippi region and in the middle west were exploited industrially on a short-term basis, just as were mines and coalpits and other raw material deposits, without any thought of renewal.

The consequences of this destruction of forest land were disastrous–a rapid run-off of precipitation in the denuded catchment area, the washing away of good soil, landslides and mudflow on slopes, inundations in the lower reaches of rivers, deposition of debris, and presently drought, steppe and desert formation over entire regions, associated in populous countries with periodic famines; destructive abundance followed by equally damaging water shortage. The Yangtse river carries 600 million tons of silt into the sea each year. Along the upper reaches of the Yellow River is the world's worst water and wind eroded region. The advance of the African sand oceans and of the Australian steppe continues. Extensive forest cutting in Central Africa led to the emergence of savannah, steppe and desert within a single generation. In the United States, three-quarters of all agriculturally utilized areas reveal damage from water or wind erosion. "One day this crime against the soil will be talked of as a piece of immense folly" (Baker).

The tragedy for mankind lies in the fact that the destruction of forests has continued for more than a thousand years without anyone being aware of it. Each human generation only knew nature as it was in its own day, without realizing its past or future. Yet the destinies of a nation are indissolubly bound up with the forest and there are many instances of the decline of great nations and ancient civilizations starting with its disappearance. Fortunately in most countries, this creeping destruction of the landscape has now begun to lead to the realization that the forest is of vital importance to a country and its people. Baker says: "We imagine that we control nature. We believe that science, chemistry and the machine are capable of solving all difficulties. Yet the startling realization is dawning on us that the achievements of the new world will wither away just as quickly as they came to us. Nature is still in command."

Changing tasks of the forest

Man has always utilized the various products of the forest–berries and wild fruit, mushrooms and fungi, wild animals and, increasingly as the population increased, timber in the form of fuelwood, structural timber and timber for processing. Unfortunately the profitability of forestry has been declining for many years and, by comparison with the higher profits of industry and transport, has been losing in importance. To defend the forest against the demands made on it we have to answer the question: What else does the forest give us? What other indispensable tasks does it fulfil?

Inhabitants of mountain valleys soon discovered that forests protected their settlements, farms and communications from numerous hazards of the mountains. Ever since men ventured into the mountains they have invariably settled in the shelter of forests and have tried to preserve this shelter by placing an interdiction on the forest belt above the villages. In these interdicted forests there was an absolute ban on any utilization because it was believed that this was the best way to preserve the forest. Realization of the protective value represented by the forest penetrated deeply into the awareness of alpine peoples.

From this concept of the interdicted forest that of the protected forest later developed. Protected forests are all those within the catchment area of unregulated waters, and all those whose location offers protection against avalanches, rock and ice falls, landslides, mud torrents and exceptional water levels. The protected forest discharges a particular function–it provides protection from natural dangers, and guards men against disaster and suffering. Most mountain valleys would not be habitable without forests.

The lowland forests do not have this special task to perform; there is no risk of avalanches, or of stone and ice falls. There, until recently, the forest's economic yield was the main consideration. Recent developments however, accelerated during the last decade or two, have suddenly changed all this. The rapid increase in population, its concentration in favored residential regions, the pace of industrialization, the increase in the number of motor vehicles by 100 to 180 times within fifty years, greater noise, feverish restlessness, exploitation of our natural water resources to their exhaustion, rapid and almost incredible pollution of waters, fouling of the air by dust and smoke and its poisoning from chemical waste gases– all these have created novel threats which are already gravely jeopardizing mankind and are bound to do so even more in the future.

Because of its various beneficial effects, the forest is in a position to banish or at least greatly diminish many of these dangers. These additional uses have been described as its "amenity function" or "welfare function" because they touch upon man's welfare in a great many ways. This trend has lent an unexpected importance to the forest in non-mountainous areas, especially in densely populated lowlands. Any forest, wherever situated, is capable of discharging beneficial and protective functions in the widest sense–protection not only against natural disasters but against the dangers created by man himself.

It is difficult to draw a strict line between protective and welfare functions. The forest's regulatory effect on water balance first of all offers protection against destruction of the soil and thus prevents disastrous floods–it therefore offers protection, in the traditional sense, against a natural danger. But the higher water level of springs and streams during dry periods, the filtration of precipitated water through the forest soil–these too are important to the water supply, i.e. to public welfare. Regeneration of the air is important not only as an amenity but for man's protection generally. These protective and welfare functions are therefore often bracketed as the "social functions" of the forest because, unlike its economic yields, they benefit not merely the owner of the forest but the community as a whole.

This is not to belittle the economic importance of the forest. It is only by furthering it that we can create the most favorable conditions for the preservation of the forest and its social functions. But today there is more at stake–the major part of the population who do not own forests but nevertheless derive the greatest benefit from them. The forest is an irreplaceable gift of nature without which our whole environment would be unthinkable and unusable.

In alpine valleys, in the course of winter or in spring, and according to the structure of the snow cover and weather conditions, avalanches are formed by snow masses which break off and slip; these descend with elemental force at a headlong pace and frequently cause extensive devastation. Since topographical conditions play an important part, these avalanches usually follow traditional paths.

Avalanches never occur within a healthy mountain forest or within an adequately stocked forest belt along the upper tree lines, because the snow cover there is stabilized and nailed down by trees and cannot start slipping. Careful maintenance of the forest, to make sure it is adequately stocked, is therefore imperative. Where avalanches formed above the treeline strike the forest below with full force, the forest cannot maintain its protection in the long run. Every avalanche will break into the forest; subsequent avalanches will widen the breach, deepen the penetration, until eventually the forest belt is pierced and the snow masses can sweep unobstructed down to the valley floor carrying with them anything in their path. The end result is the familiar picture, of a protective cover pierced by countless avalanche tracks and gulleys.

In the past the natural forest limit in the Alps was considerably higher. Along this nature-determined upper frontier the forest is engaged in a perpetual struggle against the hazards of nature. Here is the front line where resistance is offered to penetration of hostile natural forces and their advance down into the valley, into the human living space. It is a struggle of unparalleled rigor, with many trees, engaged as it were in single combat, holding out at exposed outposts, battered and torn, often mis-shapen, while others rallied in groups offer common resistance. There is an ebb and flow, with penetrations and thrusts achieved by rock falls and avalanches and a cautious groping upwards and pushing forward again by the forest in calmer periods. Here nature's laws are harder. In spite of the millions of seeds produced by the forest in generous profusion, replacement of trees is often slight. Many seeds fall on infertile rock, on snow and ice, or into precipices. Young saplings are continuously exposed to dangers and only a few among thousands grow to maturity. How incredible that man should intervene here not on the side of the forest but against it. Through continuous intensive grazing, through the clear-cutting of forests, through excessive removal of wood for the mountain-pasture economy, for mining, iron-smelting and glass-making plants, or for the maintenance of mule tracks the forest over the centuries has been almost completely destroyed in many mountain valleys, with entire slopes denuded or the natural upper tree line depressed by an average of 600 to 1,000 feet in nearly all accessible areas.

Nowhere does nature punish the disregard of its laws more severely than in mountain regions. "Snow avalanches have increased in number with progressive forest cutting and now strike in many places where previously they occurred rarely. This evil has been promoted more than anything by deforestation along the upper treeline" (E. Landolt). Heavy precipitation and melt-water have ripped open and washed away the soil denuded of its protection. Erosion has speeded up; gullies have deepened with every thunderstorm; landslides have become more frequent. Highland pastures and forests were ruined by stones and debris. Untamed high water caused serious inundations and depositions of debris in the lowlands. The climate of the mountain valleys became harsher, the land less fertile, the valleys less habitable.

These increasing threats and, more particularly, the serious damage caused by floods in the second half of the 19th century, eventually opened people's ears to the warnings which had been uttered for some time. Terrible devastation was caused by floods in September and October 1868, a few years after E. Landolt had submitted to the Swiss Federal Council his report on the state of the high alpine forests, emphasizing the progressive loss of forest, the decline in soil fertility, the increasingly frequent and ever more destructive avalanches and floods in the valleys, and after he had put forward his proposals for remedial forestry measures. Damage in the cantons of Uri, Grisons, St. Gallen, Ticino and Valais was estimated at 14 million francs. The spell was broken: the Federal Councillors discussed the question of protective barriers and forestation in the mountain valleys. In 1874 a new article of the Constitution authorized the Confederation to exercise supervision over water-regulation and forestry police in the high mountains, and 1876 saw the passage of Switzerland's first forestry law. This was a definite forest protection and policing law which, though at the time applicable only to the mountains and the foothills, had sprung from the realization that the forest must be protected if it, in turn, is to protect country and people.

Welfare functions in the wider sense

In many ways the foundations of our natural life are connected with the forest. Preservation of the forest will ensure favorable living conditions for man who is continuously affected by its welfare functions.

Forest and water: Pure water and clean air are gifts of nature which we accept without realizing how precious they are and what they mean to our lives. Supplying the population with healthy water is probably one of our most pressing tasks. The forest, with its highly favorable effect on a region's water budget and on the quality of that water, can make this task easier. "The forest is the father of rivers. Water saves the man dying of thirst and the field thirsting for moisture, but it becomes an enemy when it is not tamed and guarded by trees."

The forest soil is able to absorb precipitation and melt-water, filter it, store it and slowly release it. This beneficial action is due to the loose structure of a naturally grown and undisturbed forest soil. It represents a magnificent system of pores, major cavities and soil particles, developed over a long period of time from fallen leaves and needles, from weathered soil and from the invisible activity of countless soil organisms. The total pore space of good forest soil can amount to two-thirds of the soil volume. To work this soil would be harmful because this would destroy its peculiar complex texture, its entire internal architecture.

This looseness results in an exceptionally high permeability to water. Experiments made by the Swiss Forestry Research Institute showed that the seepage time for a 4-inch water column for arable land at Büren on the Aare was 95 minutes, while for an ancient interdicted forest with the same subsoil it was a mere 5½ minutes. In the catchment area of the Höllbach stream the same quantity of water was soaked up on waterlogged pasture land in 100 minutes, on drained pasture in 38 minutes, in a 20-year-old forest plantation in 8 minutes, and in a 40-year-old forest plantation in 3 minutes. A pasture alongside the interdicted forest at Andermatt showed a mean seepage time of over 3 hours while for the interdicted forest itself it was a mere 3 minutes.

Because of this high permeability the water reaching the forest floor, even in the event of heavy rain or very rapid thaw, penetrates almost completely into the soil, even on steep slopes, and the amount that is not evaporated through the soil or the forest stand filters into the subsoil and there feeds springs and ground water. In the open country an appreciable part of the water runs off the surface leading to high water and floods. Water draining away rapidly in valley rivers is moreover largely lost to water supplies. Prolonged investigations by Engler and Burger into drainage conditions in two side valleys of the Emmental Valley showed that, during the same period of time, about 10 per cent less water drained from the well-stocked Sperbelgraben than from the sparsely wooded Rappengraben. These figures, admittedly, do not include the portion of precipitation which seeped straight into the subterranean ground water down the valley flanks and under the debris as percolation water because the measurements were only able to register the surface run-off of the main stream.

According to American data, out of 80 inches annual precipitation a total of 56 inches or 70 per cent ran off on open ground, half of it on the surface and only 28 inches or 35 per cent as ground water; in the forest, on the other hand, 44 inches or 55 per cent of the total precipitation ran off–a mere 3.2 inches or 4 per cent on the surface and 41 inches or 51 per cent as ground water. Thus in open country only about a third of the precipitation seeped into the ground water compared with one-half in the forest.

The beneficial effect of the forest on the water budget of streams and rivers was realized by foresters and scientists long before research began to concern itself with these questions. Nature is a magnificent laboratory and countless dangerous floods in the past have impressively demonstrated the consequences of forest destruction in Switzerland. The denudation of the mountain valleys led inescapably to serious upsets of the water regime of entire river valleys. The faster the surface run-off of water, the more marked is its surface erosion. Between 1932 and 1952 the sparsely wooded Rappengraben produced on an average about three times the quantity of detritus per unit catchment area of that produced by well-wooded areas. In a wooded valley of California, where drainage measurements had previously been conducted, the surface run-off increased ten-fold and the quantity of detritus fifteen-fold after extensive forest areas had been destroyed by fires.

The best and most effective control of torrents is therefore by way of forestation of their catchment area. The cost of constructional regulation of streams is a multiple of that of forestation, without producing any effect on the amount of water carried. Forestation promotes the seepage of precipitation into the soil, an appreciable lowering of high-water peaks, a reduction in the detritus carried, and a perceptibly greater drainage during dry periods. In the forest the melting of the snow is postponed by days or weeks, which likewise contributes to a more even drainage. The improvement of low-water carriage is moreover of particular importance because seepage through the stream-bed results in a certain feeding of the ground water even in dry periods and because our rivers at low water are scarcely able to discharge their task as diluting agents for effluent. The part played by the forest in improving the quality of water can be demonstrated even more convincingly than its effect on the quantitative water balance. Considering the wealth of precipitation in Central Europe–on average 32 inches annually–there is as a rule no water shortage provided enough of it filters through to the ground water.

Forest soil, rich in humus and covered with a good layer of leaves and needles, is an excellent and efficient filter for precipitated water. This is why springs and ground water from wooded catchment areas are perfectly sound. Extensive continuous forest cover also prevents all kinds of building and hence the pollution of the water through oil or effluent. Nor is there any danger from fertilizers as on intensively farmed arable and pasture land. It is therefore imperative to afforest regular ground water zones in order to preserve the quality of the water. Such water management forests, which should be stocked exclusively with locally appropriate tree species with a high percentage of deciduous broadleaves, represent quantitatively and qualitatively the best assurance of good water.

The cleansing effect of forest soil is so marked that certain cities, such as Frankfurt and Basel, have for a number of years been letting pre-clarified river water seep through the forest floor near the ground water pumps in order thus to enrich the ground water by many hundred million gallons annually.

Klose has calculated that at a precipitation of 39.4 inches in a suitably wooded catchment area about 2,000 cubic meters more drinking water can be obtained per hectare of forest area (about 214,000 U.S. gallons per acre) because of the increased seepage and more regular drainage. At the German cost of 30 pfennig per cubic meter (about 4c per 100 U.S. gallons) this means an additional economic yield from the forest of DM 600 per hectare (about $78 per acre)–an amount which normally far surpasses the net profit from wood utilization in even the best forests.

Forest and air: Destruction of the landscape and far-reaching interference with our environment begin to increase at an alarming rate the moment settlement density and economic activity exceed a certain point. Not only the condition of our waters but that of our air has also deteriorated. In many regions air pollution is worse than is realized; the danger is that we do not see it. Every rainfall cleanses the dusty air; winds and gales effect large-scale upheavals in our atmospheric envelope and once more supply us with fresh air. We are pursuing an ostrich policy: what we do not see does not exist for us.

When we talk of air pollution we must differentiate between pollution by solid particles of dust and soot on the one hand and air poisoning from toxic gases on the other. When fuels of all types are burned, large quantities of soot and dust particles are emitted into the air in addition to waste gases. In the Ruhr there are factories which emit up to 400 tons of dust each day. The smoke-stacks of the American steel centers hurl 6,000,000 tons of coal dust into the air every year. Modern transport, in addition, results in road dirt, rubber and asphalt dust. In Munich some 7,000 tons of rubber dust from the tires of motor vehicles get into the atmosphere each year. In Los Angeles as much as 1,600 tons of incompletely combusted material are emitted into the air each day.

These solid impurities in the air result in perceptible clouding. Above the major industrial zones there hangs an almost permanent huge canopy of haze which darkens the sun and the daylight, and discolors the blue of the sky to a dull grey. In the Ruhr the incidence of sunlight is reduced up to 40 per cent by the dusty atmosphere. Below the haze layer there is a shortage of ultraviolet rays. In consequence, the incidence of cancer and tuberculosis is higher in heavy industrial regions.

The larger dust particles suspended in the air gradually settle on the ground so that incredible quantities of dirt are deposited near the dust sources. In the Ruhr dust charts have been compiled on the basis of the data obtained at over 1,700 recording points. In Düsseldorf the annual dust deposit amounts to 12 kg per 100 square meters of ground (36 ounces per square yard), at the center of the Ruhr the figure is roughly 36 kg (106 ounces). In English industrial regions dust quantities of up to 60 kg per 100 square meters (177 ounces per square yard) annually have been recorded.

Forests and parks contribute greatly in cleansing the air we breathe. The tree canopy acts as a filter which traps the dust and soot particles from passing air. Every rain washes the filter clean again and restores its absorptive capacity. Indeed, with the deciduous trees it is completely renewed by the cyclical shedding and growth of leaves. Particularly effective are tree belts, strips of forest with trees of staggered height and forests established in terraces, where the moving air passes through the foliage canopy. But even air passing over the top of forests has some of its dust particles filtered out by the more prominent treetops reaching into the airspace like tentacles, as well as by the reduction of the wind velocity because there are no air currents rising over large forest expanses and the dust therefore settles more rapidly.

According to Meldau's measurements stands of red fir and pine trap 30 to 35 tons of dust per hectare per year (12 to 14 tons per acre) and stands of beech up to 70 tons (28 tons per acre). In the Ruhr, Wentzel found black incrustations of dust several inches thick in the root area of the older forest trees, from flying ash washed down the stem.

In view of the high filtration effect of the forest canopy it is not surprising that inside the forest the air contains less dust than over open country and, more particularly over cities. According to Megamy one cubic meter (35 cubic feet) of air over industrial cities contains 100,000 to 500,000 dust and soot particles; over country towns the figure is 35,000 and in the forest 2,500. According to the dust distribution map drawn by Löbner for Leipzig in 1935, based on a smaller particle size, the air drifting over open country has a relatively slight dust content of 300,000 particles per cubic meter (8,500 per cubic foot); upon entering the city it is greatly enriched with dust, its content reaching 1.2 million (34,000 per cubic foot), or in the neighborhood of the railway station 5 million particles per cubic meter (142,000 per cubic foot), while the open green spaces in the east of the city achieve a rapid filtration, reducing the dust content to 600,000 particles per cubic meter (17,000 per cubic foot).

Excessive depositions of dust, soot and especially cement dust may damage the forest. During prolonged dry periods encrusted layers form on leaves and needles, and are only incompletely washed off by rain. In consequence, respiration, gas exchange and the incidence of light are reduced. Photosynthesis measurements on artificially dusted leaves showed losses of one-fifth to one-third, i.e. a substantial diminution of growth.

Strictly speaking, we don't need any numerical proof that a forest cleanses air in a superb manner. Don't we all draw a deep breath as we step into the hushed expanse of a forest in order to fill our lungs with fresh air rich in oxygen and poor in dust?

A more serious problem is the poisoning of air by chemical substances and waste gases from industrial and domestic heating plants, motor vehicles and chemical factories. Air pollution by a great variety of compounds of sulfur, fluorine and chlorine, by carbon monoxide and dioxide, has reached a large scale in many places. K. Wentzel quotes certain factories in the Ruhr which emit 500 tons of sulfur dioxide into the air each day. Air poisoning can produce grave damage to human health, in the form of blood poisoning, destruction of lung tissue, rickets, lung cancer and increased susceptibility to infectious diseases. The forest is virtually helpless in the face of air poisoning; indeed it suffers from it more than it can contribute to a remedy. True enough, the cells of needles and leaves possess a certain storage capacity for poisons and hence a certain detoxification potential. In the neighborhood of industrial plants the forest canopy contains double to triple the normal amount of toxic substances. But these achievements are accomplished by the forest at the expense of its own health: in the case of chronic absorption trees die even at a low gas concentration in poisoned air, and in the event of high toxicity they will die after short acute exposure. Particularly dangerous is sulfur dioxide produced by the combustion of coal and oil, which greatly reduces green plant respiration, transpiration and assimilation. Conifers are even more susceptible to air poisoning; they perish at gas concentrations which merely cause reduced growth in broadleaves. In the city forests of Duisburg which measure over 2,500 acres, the proportion of indigenous pines was formerly about 30 per cent of all trees; nowadays only 100 to 200 of this tree species survive–the rest have all been killed by smoke. In pronounced smoke-damage zones, therefore, replanting has to be done with smoke-resistant broadleaves. But even in broadleaved forests reduced growth, regeneration difficulties and considerable drops in yield have been recorded. But there is more at stake than this: in concentrated industrial areas, where the forest has to perform a variety of welfare functions, its very survival is in jeopardy.

A problem which has not so far received the attention it deserves is that of the oxygen balance of the air. All animals and plants must breathe oxygen to stay alive. But particularly large quantities are needed by coal and oil heating and by combustion engines. In Switzerland, for instance, with a population of 5.6 million, the quantity of oxygen required annually for breathing amounts to barely 2,000,000 tons. But 27 million tons are used up for technical combustion, or as much as another 81 million people would need for breathing. It has been predicted that oil consumption in Switzerland will rise from six to twelve million tons in the seventies. This would result in an excess consumption of oxygen of roughly 20 million tons or as much as a further 60 million inhabitants would need for breathing. Quite apart from the enormous quantities of toxic sulfur compounds which are emitted into the air in technical combustion, the amount of oxygen consumed is replaced by 1.4 times the quantity of poisonous carbon dioxide. Molecular oxygen, without which man, animals and plants cannot live, is supplied mainly by our green plant cover. In a magnificent process green plants use carbon dioxide from the air and water from the soil in order, with the aid of sunlight and chlorophyll, to produce starch and sugar. During this process oxygen is released in the same quantities as is needed for the combustion or breakdown of the organic compounds. Many investigations have shown that the production of solid substances and hence oxygen production by the forest is about twice to three times that of a similar area under agricultural cultivation. For the cultivated area of Switzerland, for example, it has been calculated that the green plant cover produces 22 million tons of oxygen annually as against a present consumption of 29 million tons. Switzerland thus already has an oxygen deficit of 7 million tons annually and an accretion of poisonous carbon dioxide in the atmosphere of 10 million tons. If the above mentioned acceleration in technical combustion were in fact to materialize this would mean, within ten years, a deficit of roughly 27 million tons of oxygen and an accretion of nearly 40 million tons of toxic carbon dioxide.

Naturally, since we are dealing with global processes, the oxygen balance of a single country is not decisive. Resources of oxygen in the atmosphere are still considerable and seemingly inexhaustible. But let us remember that conditions in highly industrialized countries are a good deal less favorable, that overall balance rapidly deteriorates as population, industrial production and especially technical combustion increase, that green belt areas continue to be encroached on and that in many countries forests are still ruthlessly exploited. At the moment the danger is not yet acute. But the day will come when mankind will be threatened with a shortage of oxygen in the atmosphere and an excess of carbon dioxide.

As a massive vegetation cover the forest is of inestimable and vital importance to the regeneration of the air we breathe. Every batch of woodland, however small, indeed each tree, is a dust trap for air pollution and an oxygen factory. Let us therefore spare forests and trees, and promote replanting on a larger scale.

Forest and recreation: Around 1900 some 22 per cent of the Swiss population lived in localities with more than 10,000 inhabitants. By 1920 the percentage had risen to 28, by 1941 to 33 and by 1960 to 42. If the trend continues on this scale nearly three-fifths of the population will be living in localities of urban character by the end of the century. In such metropolitan areas people are exposed in a greater measure to noise, hustle and unrest, to a continuous psychological and physical strain, to stress and overstimulation, combined with a lack of exercise. Walking and open-air activities are thus becoming ever more important. Rest and relaxation only once a year, for three or four weeks of vacation, are not enough. Maintenance of health, happiness and efficiency increasingly requires regular short-term relaxation in the evening or at weekends. This need not be concentrated in forests or open country near the major settlement zones. Present day transportation enables a large number of people to visit even remote forests so long as they are easily accessible.

The recreational effect of the forest is of particular value. Coming from the noise, traffic, hustle and bustle, dust and foul air to the unfading beauty and tranquility of the forest, with its pleasing greenery, with its right to forsake the paths and wander between the trees, the visitor knows that now he has left his daily routine behind him. He is struck by the magnificent living community of the forest with its permanence and harmony, which impresses him the more human society is riven by quarrel, tensions, hatred and war. He delights in aimless wandering along lonely paths, along secret trails with countless surprises and numerous greater and lesser miracles. How fascinating and striking is the change of the seasons, the bursting of delicate leaves in spring, the luxuriant wealth of the deep green in the summer, the brilliant colors of the fall, then the dropping of leaves as nature gets ready for its rest, and the great silence that lies over the forest in winter. The forest is full of secrets and beauty, a real contrast to our daily impatience and hard straight paved roads.

What we seek in the forest is tranquility and silence. It is an escape from noise and bustle. In the solitude of the forest we discover ourselves again. We experience a sense of security, of being shielded against what is alien and grating in our daily lives. For a short span we also seek freedom from the compulsion of time, from deadlines and obligations. We unwind again, we draw a deep breath, we realize with surprise that work, success or failure, making money or indulging in pleasures, are not the most important things in life; some superiority is shed, some hates and anger evaporate, some anxieties disappear. We return with new courage to resume and continue the tasks which destiny has assigned to us or which we have ourselves undertaken or formulated.

In principle appropriate management of the forest will promote its protective and welfare functions simultaneously. Nevertheless, additional measures are called for in heavily frequented areas to enable the forests to discharge their recreational tasks better still–such as the marking of trails, the laying out of rest and play areas, fire fighting points, shelters, drinking fountains and tasteful development of spots with a beautiful view. But care is needed not to overdo this and lay out places for festivities and public entertainment and so ruin the forest as a place for relaxation, calm and solitude, or deprive it of its natural harmony. Forests near big cities should not become overcrowded parks.

The forest and the experience of nature are indispensable to man's physical and mental health. Anybody is free to go to the forest and walk in it–with the exception of fenced-off or marked protected cultivation areas. Yet the regular use of the forest in heavily visited areas and the ensuing damage done to the forest frequently exceeds what a proprietor may reasonably be expected to accept. If we have to protect the forest for man we must in turn frequently protect it against man. Education and guidance must help people to enjoy nature but also to practice consideration, decency and respect for the forest and nature generally.

Forest and landscape: Next to topography and natural water the forest is probably the most stable and impressive element in our landscape. It gives it its characteristic appearance. To quote Eidmann: "Relief by itself is dead; only the forest cover gives it life."

The distribution of forest and fields of a typical landscape has evolved over the centuries. It is entirely natural that agriculture should have laid claim to the better soils and orographically more favorable situations. The forest was left with less favorable features such as dry hilltops, steep slopes, beds of streams, waterlogged and slippery ground and sunless northern slopes. There is therefore a close connection between topography, settlement and forest cover.

Forest clearance was probably the most decisive interference ever made in a natural landscape and one which resulted in enduring change. The spread of settlement areas, industrialization, the development of major residential centers and of modern communications continues to transform the landscape on a major scale. Our machine age has been adding new features to our landscape by the removal or piling up of hills, the creation of artificial reservoirs, water utilization, large-scale dredging of gravel, quarrying, and major construction projects. But all these are dwarfed by the forest cover which clothes mountains and valleys. Changes in this forest cover through clearance affect the landscape more gravely; in less wooded regions even the clearance of minor patches of woodland, spinneys and ribbons of trees along streams has a disturbing effect. Preservation of the present forest distribution is of major importance for the appearance of our landscape. It is not enough therefore for cleared forests to be replaced by forestation elsewhere. We cannot simply move a forest from one place to another. Apart from the fact that forest clearance abruptly destroys an existing living community so that its protective and welfare functions are diminished for decades to come, all this would be an intolerable interference with the familiar face of our country.

The forest is also an important element in regional planning. Topography, water and forest represent a solid framework for the utilization of our environment. Once we upset this framework our entire plan is in danger of collapsing. The forest is the still center in a headlong development. Even if the rapidly swelling ocean of houses floods the open country, engulfing the forests or flowing between them, reaching out far into open spaces, where it encounters the forest it is forced to halt. The forest is the most effective, cheapest and most permanent fencing strip for residential and industrial areas. If such green belt and recreational areas had to be artificially created not even the richest municipality would now be in the financial position to realize even a small fraction of them. From the planning point of view it is imperative that the present distribution of forests be preserved.

Protection against noise: Industrial and traffic noise has intensified enormously with industrialization and motorization and has so extended its duration that it scarcely ever ceases even at night. Since the turn of the century real noise has increased a thousand times. Excessive noise can reduce a man's work performance, intensify his irritability and friction with others, and even damage his health.

Noise can be reduced by planting a stand of trees. Of course one must not expect that narrow strips of trees, just because they conceal the sound source optically, are sufficient to contain the noise to any appreciable extent. A major reduction of noise can be achieved only by wide forest belts. This noise protection is most effective if trees are planted in parallel echelons, producing turbulence of sound waves. Measurements have shown that a forest belt a hundred yards wide, with thick undergrowth, can reduce the maximum noise normal on major highways down to half or one-quarter, or to the mean noise values of light traffic areas. Forest belts and larger stands of trees thus provide a desirable and indispensable boundary strip between predominantly residential zones and noisy industrial and traffic installations.

Protection against wind: Although protection against wind is not as important in Switzerland as it is in the vast denuded regions of many overseas countries, its value is nevertheless realized in Europe. A strip of forest or a spinney acts as a wind barrier and produces an air cushion which greatly reduces the wind velocity compared with a neighboring field. The same effect is observed in the lee of a forest. One only has to step into a forest from open country on a windy winter's day to experience a feeling of entering a calm room.

172

In whatever country major forest areas have been liquidated the destruction of the soil by wind is well-known. During dry periods the crumbly surface, mainly of light soils, is turned to dust and carried off by the wind, often over great distances. Shifting dunes are piled up, and these advance inexorably, swallowing up forests and open country.

It was the Russians who first planted wind shelter belts in the wide steppe and desert areas of Central Asia, in the early 19th century, and achieved astonishing success with them. In America, too, the Soil Conservation Service has taken in hand forestation in catchment areas of large rivers and the planting of thousands of miles of wind shelter belts in order to halt the erosion of the soil by water and wind.

Switzerland has benefited from planted forest belts in the Rhine Valley at St. Gallen, in the Rhône Valley and in the Valley of the Orbe. On the windward side this effect is observed over up to five to ten times the height of the forest or shelter belt, and on the leeward side as far as 20 to 30 times the height. Most effective are belts with a medium permeability, which allow the wind to pass through while retarding it sufficiently. Excessively close, impermeable forest belts cause the wind to leap over the forest, leading to dangerous air turbulence. In the shelter of forests and trees dew formation is increased, soil desiccation is less, and the yield of cultivated farmland is increased. The forest, therefore, not only protects the soil on which it actually stands but also reduces desiccation and wind erosion over a wide radius of open country. Villages and settlements in exposed areas have always sought the shelter of nearby forests.

The population will continue to grow, settlements and motorization will spread, the number of motor vehicles will increase, consumption of water will go up, noise and hustle will get worse, technology will gradually engulf all spheres of life. Preservation of clean air and water will become more difficult in spite of all measures, and it will become more urgent as the danger outstrips our counter-measures. A high standard of living has to be paid for. Modern ideas of utilization are marked by a lack of responsibility and concern. Mankind's spiritual growth has clearly not kept pace with technological progress and material prosperity. It is especially in the highly developed countries that ethical maturity seems to be declining.

Ensuring sound water, clean air, and tranquility for the future is becoming an increasingly pressing task. The forest can help us to solve it. In the face of the alarming threat to the basis of our existence, our conscience and our obligation to a remote future compel us to mobilize the entire public in earnest defense of the forest against ever more numerous plans for further clearance. We must do so today; tomorrow may be too late. The struggle for the forest has become everyone's cause.

Forest clearance and profiteering

Top-quality woodland in Europe under present conditions has a yield value of, at the most, DM 4,000 to 5,000 per hectare ($520 to $650 per acre), and poor woodlands only half or one-quarter of this figure. The same land could be sold as building land in a city for DM 100 to 200 per square meter, i.e. for DM 1,000,000 to 2,000,000 per hectare ($130,000 to $260,000 per acre). This huge discrepancy lies at the heart of the problem of forest clearance. To cut down a forest in order to provide building land is profiteering.

The threat to the forest begins at the point where a competent authority issues a clearance permit to the owner of woodland and thereby enables him to realize several hundred times the value of his land by turning it into building land. But where does the threat stop? What barrier can be erected to check such activities? On grounds of equity, must not other owners of woodland be allowed to convert their forests into building land as well? This would leave the door wide open to wholesale clearance: woodland, hitherto largely unaffected, would become the object of unlimited speculation and in the neighborhood of settlements the forest would be lost. True enough, the forest is the property of its owner–perhaps a municipality, perhaps a private person. But this does not mean that he can dispose of it as he likes–landscape, nature, air and water, the country, indeed everything connected with the forest–all these belong to the whole nation which has a prior claim to the preservation of good water, clean air, protection from noise, and which derives so much recreation and happiness from it that the proprietor of the forest must accept a limitation of his right of disposal for the sake of the general public.

Clearance control is the most important means to ensure a country's sound forest policy. It should not be weak in its confrontation with those interested in diverting woodlands to different uses. Forest clearance results in losses which cannot be offset by *any* economic gains; there is no doubt that the main importance of the forest has been inexorably shifting from economic yield to protective and welfare effects. It is certainly not enough to justify forest clearance by the argument that the applicant is carrying out a replacement forestation on at least the same area elsewhere. Quite apart from the fact that a forest association cannot be built up in a new location overnight, this would also mean an inadmissible shift of the forest from settlement zones to remote regions. A glance at regional trends already reveals a decline in forest area in main settlement zones, which are poorer in forest anyway, and an increase in more densely wooded regions away from inhabited localities. Any forest clearance near a residential area means a loss of forest amenities for the inhabitants, a loss which cannot be compensated by forestation programs in remote areas.

As a general principle forest clearance can now only be considered in cases where important public interest is involved, an interest which clearly outweighs the public interest in forest preservation. Unfortunately such a public interest in forest clearance is far too readily claimed by municipalities, associations or state bodies. On closer examination these wishes usually reveal considerations of usefulness or convenience or even financial considerations which, in the long run, are not as important as the preservation of the forest.

A difficult and thankless task of the forestry service is the prevention of the gradual encroachment on forests in the immediate contact zone between settlement and private forests. By way of minor projects, car parks, laying out of lawns, children's playgrounds or recreational areas, or by extending gardens into an abutting forest, step by step its edge is broken up. Yet preservation of the protective forest edge is necessary for the climate within the forest; it is also the best insurance for the continuous existence of the forest which will otherwise be gradually forced back. To restore a forest edge once it has been lost and to re-establish its drainage and protective effect by way of planting or maintenance usually takes a long time–50 years or more. In the meantime the forest area behind it will have suffered grave damage from sunlight and desiccation.

Building chalets or weekend houses inside the forest should likewise be avoided. In most cases they involve such ancillary services as car parks, playgrounds and woodsheds, all in the surrounding forest. In consequence, the forest is loosened up in a way that prevents it from discharging its task and may even cause it gradually to disappear altogether.

In addition to preserving existing forests it is necessary to restock denuded mountain flanks and to raise the upper tree limit where it lies too low. Of course in the mountains there will always be damage from natural causes; the forest's protective action is not absolute. Reforesting breaches caused by avalanches or by torrents is one of the most important measures to ensure the forest's protective functions. But this is a difficult and costly enterprise. At these denuded spots, which at one time were forests, new stands are helplessly exposed to many dangers–rock-falls and snowdrifts, wash-out and landslides, sharp fluctuations between dry hot summers and extremely cold winters. The margin between success and failure is very small. The costs involved in re-establishing a protective forest, which usually involves construction of roads and protective barriers, are colossal. The dense population of the lowland, who equally benefit from these measures and to whom the mountain valleys are available as ideal vacation and recreation areas, have an obligation to support such programs.

One threat to the forest today is that its economic yield is declining all the time while maintenance costs are rising; in areas of difficult access forests already show a deficit. Not unreasonably many a private owner of woodland asks himself why he should keep and maintain his forest and invest money in it when he might collect large sums by utilizing it as building land. He finds it hard to understand that the public interest in preservation of the forest should take precedence over his private needs. This fact imposes a duty on the general public to assist the woodland proprietor in the special difficulties he has in managing his forest–by subsidies for road construction, promotion of fuelwood sales through the installation of combined oil and wood heating plants in large public buildings or in district heating plants for subsidized large-scale settlements, by an increased use of wood in interior decoration and for furniture, and by tax relief for the forest owner. In Europe 54 per cent of all forests are privately owned. Of these, 50 per cent are owned by farmers and thus represent a substantial portion of the livelihood of rural households. Only where forests are not suitable for normal economic management, as for instance in the high mountains or within metropolitan areas, should the state or the municipalities be given the right of pre-emption.

Forest or desert

Mankind has gained much from the progress of economy and transport, from technological development and a higher standard of living. Have we not also lost something? Have we not gained much that we have paid for dearly? We have lost clean water, contemplation, tranquility; we are about to lose also our clean air; we have changed the familiar face of our country, often for the worse, and we have thoughtlessly sacrificed much natural beauty.

The demands made on the forest today are greater than ever. To produce an economic yield and simultaneously to discharge its increasingly important protective and welfare functions are not mutually exclusive tasks. On the contrary, the two functions can be simultaneously discharged given a forest management based on local natural conditions.

In largely denuded regions huge sums of money are invested in recreating forests for their beneficial effects. Matters are a great deal simpler in a country where forests still exist. They merely have to be looked after and defended against countless demands.

Society in our industrial age is increasingly dependent on the social functions of the forest. Only if we succeed, in spite of extending residential areas and industrial regions, in preserving our forests on a sufficient scale and in sound condition, can our indispensable environmental basis be assured. The history of numerous countries presents us with a categorical alternative–forest or desert.

92 Young beech foliage *(Fagus silvatica)* flooded with sunlight
93 Silky-haired seed of traveler's joy *(Clematis vitalba)* ▷
94 Male fern *(Dryopteris filix-mas)* ▷▷

Why is it that many countries, especially those with a high standard of living, treat the natural basis of their existence with such irresponsibility? Man has his eye on short-term profit. We only think of today, and life today is still very good in many countries. The economy is running at full speed, earnings are high; there are still extensive recreational areas, enough usable drinking water, the air is still fit to be breathed. And it will be the same tomorrow. But what will things be like in the next century if reckless exploitation and destruction continue? And after that? Foresters are used to taking the long view. In the forest it takes more than a century, in mountain forests several centuries, before a tree is mature and ready for cutting. That is why they often cast their eyes a long way back since the stock utilized at present originated in the last century or earlier still. But they also look far into the future because many silvicultural measures, many replacement plantations, will not produce a yield until the next century or later. This awareness of the endurance of what is happening and being planned today, this sense of responsibility towards a distant future, should guide all men in their actions and omissions to a much greater extent and become a guideline for their attitude to nature, landscape and country.

In April 1946, at the Second World Charter Forestry luncheon in London, attended by representatives of numerous countries, the chairman, Lord Sempill, proposed a resolution which was unanimously adopted for transmission to the United Nations: "That, realizing in face of the present world famine the dependence of Man on trees and forests, and, seeing the forests disappearing and the deserts encroaching on the remaining food sources at a rate of up to 30 miles per year on 1,000 mile fronts in three continents, this gathering of national representatives of 24 countries requests the aid of UNO in the preparation of a World Charter for Forestry."

The countries of central Europe, where a positive attitude to the forest exists, may well have to play a decisive part in this task. The principal demand would have to be: protection of the forest for the protection of man.

95 Moss carpet in a dense coniferous wood

99 Haircap moss
   (Polytrichum commune)
   in the Muota Valley,
   Switzerland

100 *Cladonia* lichen in the Chall-area of the Jura, Switzerland *(Cladonia pyxidata)*
101 *Cladonia* lichen in the Chall-area of the Jura *(Cladonia pyxidata)*
102 Club moss *(Lycopodium selago)* in the Muota Valley, Switzerland ▷
103 Moss with spore capsules on a tree stump ▷▷

108 Sulfur-yellow polypore *(Polyporus sulphureus)* with console-shaped short-stalked fruiting body

109 *Russula rosacea* or *lepida*, in oak and beech woods
110 *Calocera viscosa* on spruce stumps and splintered timber

111 Fly agaric *(Amanita muscaria)* in birch and fir forest
112 *Geastrum rufescens*, an earth-star, in coniferous and broadleaved forest

Forest Plants, Shrubs, Fungi and Berries

Peter Grünig

The forest is a multi-layered living community in which all creatures–higher plants and animals as much as animal and plant micro-organisms–discharge a multiplicity of functions. The structure of such a biological community is based on countless interrelations and dependencies and is so complex and involved that science has so far succeeded only in identifying and explaining a small part of all connections and relationships. That is why the forest is still full of wonders and mysteries to the scientist and it almost seems as if man will never succeed in snatching all its secrets from it.

A forest is far more than a mere agglomeration of various trees; it is a highly and elaborately organized manifestation of life in which all organisms, large and small, have a meaningful place. In its ideal state this biological community is in balance, subject to only slow imperceptible changes, but now and again natural events occur, triggered by catastrophic causes, upsetting the natural balance of the biological community. Forest fires, started by lightning, or large-scale destruction through wind can cause havoc in primeval forests and introduce dissonance into a harmony evolved over centuries. After such catastrophes the regeneration of the forest starts in a natural way and without human help–with the result that sooner or later, sometimes only after centuries, the original biological balance is restored. Man has introduced into his forest species of trees not placed there by nature, and for economic reasons allowed them considerable space; he has also interposed himself into its actual life cycle in the belief that he can control it according to his will. All these human interventions have drawn appropriate responses from the forest. Wherever they have run counter to nature soil fertility has declined or stands have been attacked by various diseases or pests. Planted forests are far more prone to wind and snow damage than natural forests. The dangers threatening forests too extensively controlled by man can be countered by making allowance in forest management for the laws of nature and by trying to shape such forests to fall as much in line as possible with natural forests in terms of tree species and structure. The modern forest manager tries not to interfere with the forest's natural environment. He therefore tends to reject artificial planting and clear-cutting, which lead to unnatural stands, and to cooperate with the natural cycles of the forest. The naturally developing forest means maximum productivity qualitatively and quantitatively in the long run, and this concept requires modern forestry practice.

Plant sociology and local factors

A nature-oriented silviculture means that the concept of location has moved into the foreground of forestry. By location we mean the sum total of all external factors affecting a particular spot. Such location factors include geographical situation, altitude, exposure, general and local climate, soil conditions, and human and animal intervention as well. A location unites all nature-given prerequisites of plant growth. The various location factors can be controlled and changed by man to varying degrees. Altitude, exposure and general climatic conditions must be seen as constants; the micro-climatic conditions or the soil, and more particularly light, can be influenced by man, up to a point, by modification of the environment; i.e. soil cultivation, fertilization, irrigation, drainage, etc. While agriculture makes extensive use of these possibilities, forestry is fairly restricted in this respect by natural and economic reasons. Only light can be modified by appropriate intervention. Forestry is therefore largely dependent on the natural conditions of location and must adapt its production to it.

The two principal aids in this respect are soil science and plant sociology. Both these sciences are still very young. But already their findings have resulted in considerable successes in silviculture over the past few decades and provided this formerly empirical practice with a scientific foundation. It is impossible within the space of this book to deal with soil science in any detail, but we can take a somewhat closer look at the nature of plant sociology.

Plant sociologists divide the earth's vegetation cover into easily comprehensible and identifiable units. Anyone who has wandered attentively through fields and forests will have noticed that each location displays a certain grouping of plant species and that some plant species thrive only in very definite locations. The attentive observer will not expect to find the Arolla pine, *Pinus cembra,* or the alpenrose, *Rhododendron ferrugineum,* in the lowlands of Central Europe but in the Alps at altitudes above 5,000 feet, nor, on the other hand, will he look for the common or forest oak, *Quercus robur,* the winter lime, *Tilia cordata,* the wood crowfoot or goldilocks, *Ranunculus auricomus,* or the ground ivy, *Glechoma hederaceum,* of mixed deciduous forests in the alpine regions but in the valleys. The specific behavior of different plant species allows us to conclude that each makes quite definite demands on its environment, demands which are specific with one species and vague with another. Species with similar locational demands associate in the same location, provided rivalry between the species permits this. All species of one location together form a plant community, or rather a plant association, which is found again in similar composition wherever the same conditions exist. The plant sociologist tries to identify these recurring plant groupings, to define them and differentiate them from one another, and from them draw conclusions about the decisive location factor. Plant sociology makes it possible to gain an insight into the symbiosis of various plant species and to discover which of them find particularly favorable conditions in a certain location. It is hardly surprising, then, that this science has opened up entirely new paths to the silviculturist anxious and indeed obliged to co-operate with nature.

If we want to do justice to the phenomenon we call the forest we must view it as a biological entity with all its multiple interrelationships. But in order to get some clear ideas about these infinitely numerous connections, science is compelled to set aside the synoptic view and investigate individual aspects which can subsequently be integrated into the overall picture. To that end the plant sociologist subdivides the ecological system of the forest. A forest association is as a rule divided into the tree layer, the shrub layer and the moss layer. Although this subdivision is somewhat crude it is entirely sufficient for most purposes. Before taking a closer look at these various layers it should again be emphasized–bearing in mind the need for an integrated view–that these layers do not simply co-exist without interrelations but that in fact very definite interdependencies exist between them. Thus the density of the tree layer canopy plays a most decisive part in the constitution of the shrub, herbaceous and moss layers. To cite an example: in a dense beechwood the light conditions are often so unfavorable that few shrubs, herbaceous plants, grasses or mosses can live in it. In an open pinewood, on the other hand, conditions are more favorable for the development of luxuriant and varied shrub and herbaceous layers. In other words, each stand of trees has a specific effect on the incidence, successful growth and appearance of the vegetation associated with it.

Moss layers and lichen species

The mosses are rather insignificant children of nature, scarcely ever given their due by man. And yet there is great variety and beauty hidden in the moss carpet. Each springy moss cushion resembles the forest itself in miniature. We find here repeated on a reduced scale all forms of trees, the highest living things on earth. Thus the *Polytrichum* species are almost exact small editions of our spruces; the splendid feather-moss, *Hylocomium splendens,* resembles a cedar; the treelike feather-moss, *Climacium dendroides,* is reminiscent of a spherical tree; and the species of the genus *Thuidium* can with some justification be likened to the arborvitae. Within the great biological community of the forest a clump of moss forms a self-sufficient little world teaming with minute creatures. Tiny insects are hidden here, algae find favorable conditions in the permanent humidity, and swarms of all kinds of other creatures inhabit this dwarf world–in this respect, too, a faithful copy of the forest. In spite of their small size the mosses play a part in the forest's social budget that should not be underrated. Their often dense clumps store up precipitation; they act like small reservoirs capable of supplying water to other creatures in times of drought, and a thick moss carpet protects the structurally vulnerable forest soil from desiccation, leaking out and washing away. Moss cushions are also important in the natural rejuvenation of the forest; delicate and perishable tree saplings often establish themselves within or on the edge of these clumps as they find particularly favorable conditions for germination and growth during the early phases of life there. Time and again one is surprised and fascinated by the multiple tasks discharged within the pattern of a forest's life by these neglected mossy plants. Their destruction causes the wrecking of a rich life cycle, the extinction of a hundred forms of life. The wanderer striding over a moss carpet would do well to ponder these facts–but he is mostly ignorant of them. Respect for life begins at this minute level.

Many species of moss are firmly linked with definite types of forest. Hence the composition of the moss layer in broadleaved forests is substantially different from that in coniferous forests. Light conditions also have a marked effect on the incidence of moss. Excessively dense or excessively open stands tend to be hostile to moss, whereas average close forests with a large proportion of indirect light near ground level are regarded as favorable. For the forester mosses are important soil indicators; from them he can judge the quality of the location. Good soil conditions are suggested, for instance, by the species of *Mnium*, by *Eurhynchium stratum, Catharinaea undulata,* and *Thuidium tamariscinum.* Less valuable soils in forestry terms, on the other hand, support *Sphagnum* species, *Mastigobrym trilobatum, Hylocomium schreberi* and *Dicranum scoparium.* Mosses frequently also settle on stones, old stumps, exposed roots and sometimes even on the bark of living trees, but their combination of species differs clearly from the ones on the forest floor. It would go too far to describe all these interesting and varied associations. However, among the lower plants, mention must be made of the lichens. They too belong to the biological community of the forest and like the mosses settle on stumps, stones, tree bark or the soil, where they are capable of forming their own associations. The lichens are cryptogamous plants whose bodies are composed of algae and fungi in intimate union (symbiosis); they can attain considerable age. Among the numerous species the best known are the Iceland moss, *Cetraria islandica,* and the Lapland or reindeer moss, *Cladonia rangiferina,* both of them lichens which in the Far North serve as human and animal food and are of great economic importance; others are the large family of *Graphidaceae* and, above all, the *Usneaceae,* the whisker-like lichens frequently found in humid mountainous locations where, in their hundreds and thousands, they grow as epiphytes on trees.

Herbaceous plants, orchids and fungi

We leave these curiously attractive and strange forms of life to move on to the second level of the forest, the herbaceous layer. Here, too, we can of course only choose a few of the great multiplicity of forms. Fundamentally all plants are children of light. Without adequate light plant growth is impossible. That is why a richer herbaceous vegetation is found in open forests than in close stands, and since older stocks usually let more light through than younger ones the herbaceous layer in the latter is relatively poor compared with the multiplicity of species and individuals in the former. Everyone knows those dense young spruce stands where, apart from a few clumps of moss, the soil is covered only with dry brown needles. Lack of light at ground level prevents the growth of grasses, herbaceous plants and ferns. A totally different picture is offered by an old deciduous forest, especially in early spring. There the ground is covered with the brilliant star flowers of the wood anemone, *Anemone nemorosa,* with the red and blue flowers of the lungwort, *Pulmonaria officinalis,* or with the golden celandine, *Ranunculus ficaria.* Among the pale yellow cowslips, *Primula veris,* the strange hood of the cuckoo-pint, also known as lords and ladies, *Arum maculatum,* may peep from the colorful carpet of flowers, and many modest species of carex, *Carex spec. div.,* hasten to get their flowers pollinated. Indeed, all these plants are in a hurry because their propagation must be concluded before the leaves burst from the shrubs and broadleaved trees which shelter and guard them. The bursting of the leaves means, for this light-hungry group, the onset of shade and hence the lean period. The plant sociologist is well aware of these connections and therefore refers to the spring, summer and fall phases of a plant association. No doubt the spring phase is the most joyous to man–after the cold season a seemingly dead nature awakens with almost elemental force, producing a multitude of flowers which give huge pleasure to the naturalist and to the botanist. Later, as the sun rises higher, the forest quiets down. The birdsong falls silent towards summer and only the insects, especially the bees, fill the mysterious quiet with their buzzing. The air vibrates with heat and is fragrant with resin. This is the season more than any other when man feels quite humble in the forest. Maybe this is the sensation which poets have in mind when they speak of the mysterious inner life of the forest. At any rate, summer is also a period of quiet flowering–no longer vast carpets of flowers but individual plants which please and delight by their colors. There is the blue or purple columbine, *Aquilegia vulgaris,* which raises its delicate, curiously shaped blooms towards the light in the less dark spots of the forest, or the fragrant Turk's cap lily, *Lilium martagon,* which displays its splendor in hidden places and whose flowers suggest a turban–hence its name.

Particularly delightful are the orchid species which are not too rare in forests. With the exception of the coveted lady's slipper, *Cypripedium calceolus* (whose protection must be absolutely insisted upon if its eventual extinction is to be prevented), the orchids of Central Europe cannot match their tropical relatives in magnificence of size or color. But looking closely at the individual small blooms on the spike, perhaps under a magnifying glass, we shall discover in the European strains an unexpected, astonishing and rich beauty. Most species native to Central Europe are denizens of the open field, of grassland and pasture, and only a few venture into the twilight of the forest. But it is these very species which lend the summer forest their special color accents. Perhaps our most beautiful forest orchid is the red helleborine, *Cephalanthera rubra;* its relatively large flowers, ranging from pink to purple, are arranged in loose spikes and are strongly reminiscent of tropical orchids in color and shape. Other ornaments of the beechwood in early summer are the large white helleborine or egg orchid, *Cephalanthera damasonium,* and the two-leaved lesser butterfly orchid, *Platanthera bifolia.* Among the orchids there is also the bird's nest orchid, *Neottia nidus-avis;* this possesses no chlorophyll, either in its stem or its scale-shaped leaves, and is thus, unlike green plants, unable to assimilate or build up organic substance on its own. The bird's nest orchid is a saprophyte feeding on decomposing organic matter. Plants which feed at the expense of others, which are dependent on the consumption of living organic substance, are known as parasites. Another saprophyte among the orchids is the delicate coralroot, *Corallorhiza trifida,* a native principally of sub-alpine spruce forests.

All orchid species depend for their nutrition on the help of fungi. Between fungi and orchids there exists a very intimate symbiotic association which must be established as early as during the germination of the dustgrain-sized orchid seeds. This association between orchid and fungus is accomplished in the roots in the form of the mycorrhiza; a stable equilibrium must develop between the two symbiotic partners. This dependence of the orchids on their root fungi is the principal cause of the difficulties encountered in orchid cultivation. It is probably also the decisive obstacle to a successful transplant of orchids from their natural habitat into a garden. Let us therefore leave these attractive plants in their natural environment, where they will find the fungus they require. This is the best service we can render to the preservation of nature.

According to recent scientific investigations, forest trees also depend on fungi to a considerable extent. They too must have an intimate mutual relationship with the root fungi if they are to thrive vigorously, especially at an early age. Thus no fewer than 116 different species of mycorrhiza fungi live symbiotically with the Scotch pine, *Pinus silvestris.* Scientists still know far too little about these highly interesting symbioses. Intensive research into these multiple relationships will undoubtedly yield important results for practical forest management.

To this day, even in our technological age, fungi are to many of us the most mysterious and uncanny of forest denizens. Why is this so? Is it the poisonous character of some species? Is it their almost incredible rate of growth? Or is it perhaps a survival of ideas rooted deep in antiquity and in the Middle Ages and associated with witchcraft? Probably a little of each. As chlorophyll-less plants the fungi lead a mostly saprophytic existence, feeding on dead organic matter, or a parasitic one, feeding on living organic matter. Either in the ground or in the host plant, almost invariably hidden from man's eyes, they form a fungoid tissue, the mycelium. This consists of numerous threads, the hyphae. In favorable environmental conditions, for instance after a warm and damp summer, the mycelium abruptly produces sporophores which push through the ground, often overnight, to appear in the familiar shape of mushrooms. It is thus only a small part of the fungus plant which becomes visible and which is sought by the gourmet. The sporophore serves the propagation of the fungus because it is there that the spores ripen; these subsequently germinate and form hyphae.

Fungi play an important part in the total forest budget. We have already mentioned the importance of mycorrhiza formation. Moreover, numerous species are capable in conjunction with an army of soil bacteria and other soil creatures of breaking down fallen leaves and needles and making the nutrients contained in them once more utilizable by other plants and trees. Some species of fungi, however, are parasites and are among the most feared tree and wood pests. Who has not walked through a forest in autumn and observed the numerous sporophores of the Hallimasche, also known as honey fungus, forester's curse or fir-tree gangrene, *Armillaria mellea,* sprout from a spruce stem? Such a tree is seriously diseased and sooner or later doomed to die. Nearly all tree rot, whether of the living or dead wood, is due to fungus infection. Lower forms of fungi, on the other hand, frequently cause leaf diseases, such as mildew in oak, needle-drop in pines and larches, or witches' broom in spruces and firs, as well as cankers in numerous other tree species. The multiplicity of forms and brilliant color of the fruit receptacles of many fungi make the nature lover forget these rather disagreeable characteristics. The forester, however, must take serious account of their pathogenic properties and, chiefly through a suitable choice of species and various other biological measures, prevent their excessive spread since chemical extermination of the pests is only possible in exceptional cases, and only applicable in young forests.

Mention should be made of a particularly strange phenomenon which has at all times given rise to a variety of curious explanations–the fairy ring. Many species of fungi display the striking ability to make their numerous sporophores appear simultaneously, arranged in a circle; this is often connected with magic or witchcraft but has an entirely natural explanation. Starting from the germinating spore as its center, the mycelium spreads through a suitable forest soil and, unless it encounters in it some major ob-

202

stacle, will do so evenly in all directions. In consequence a circular mycelium disc is first formed; with advancing age the central portion of the fungoid growth dies off and all that is left in the ground is a living mycelium ring, often of considerable diameter. Whenever sporophore formation begins the hoods of the fungi break through the ground in a circle–the mysterious fairy ring.

Ferns, grasses and clearing flora

Reminiscent of bishops' croziers, ferns open their fronds in late spring; these are sometimes arranged with almost geometrical precision in magnificent funnels. Most ferns show a certain predilection for half-shaded spots where the air or the soil is damp; wherever these conditions are met and development is not restricted by excessively dense undergrowth they may emerge as the dominant species, frequently together with the (by then faded) woodruff, *Asperula odorata,* the delicate wood sorrel or shamrock, *Oxalis acetosella,* or the dead nettle, *Lamium galeobdolon.* Occasionally a profusion of ferns lends our temperate forests a touch of tropical luxuriance. This can be the case particularly in the humidity of ravines, where real fern associations may frequently evolve. Alongside the summer-green male and lady ferns *Dryopteris filix-mas* and *Athyrium filix-femina,* as well as the Austrian shield fern, *Dryopteris austriaca,* one is attracted by the evergreen lobed shield fern, *Dryopteris lobata,* the magnificent hart's tongue fern, *Phyllitis scolopendrium,* which do not look like ferns at all, and the common polypody, *Polypodium vulgare.* Among Central European ferns the bracken, *Pteridium aquilinum,* grows to impressive heights of often over 6 feet.

Ferns propagate in a rather strange manner. Although everyone knows the spores form on the underside of the ferns, it is less commonly known that these spores, which are often confused with seeds, do not directly develop into ferns; the germinating spore first forms a delicate little plant, the prothallium, which does not look like a fern but like moss and which clings flat to the ground. This prothallium carries male and female sex organs, and only after fertilization can the young fern develop from it.

The summer forest is also rich in species of grasses and grass-like plants, *Gramineae* and *Cyperaceae.* In contrast to meadows, where individual grasses are scarcely noticeable, forest grasses appear individually, each with its own personality. One of the most beautiful species is the European limegrass, *Elymus europaeus,* which attains a height of over three feet and is found in beechwoods; it possesses long slender ears with many spires; in the dry state these ears can sometimes survive the winter. Equally impressive is the giant fescue-grass, *Festuca gigantea,* in mixed broadleaved forests. The nodding melick grass *Melica nutans,* on the other hand, is remarkable not for its size but for its delicate appearance. Another very pretty grass is millet-grass, *Milium effusum,* easily recognized by its upright regular but very loose spikes. Among the family of *Cyperaceae* a species striking for its size is the great pendulous sedge, *Carex pendula,* with its almost lily-like dark green leaves; it is found in damp locations. Widespread also are wood sedge, *Carex silvatica,* fingered sedge, *Carex digitata,* with its purple leaf-sheaths, hairy sedge, *Carex pilosa,* and alpine sedge, *Carex brizoides,* large quantities of which were formerly used as upholstery material. In partially cleared forests and in artificial stands alpine sedge forms dense coarse lawns over large areas and thus represents a serious danger to forest regeneration. Mention should finally be made of the great hairy woodrush, *Luzula silvatica,* which grows in shade or half shade and in large, vigorous rich-green patches at higher altitudes, while its more graceful relation, the field woodrush, *Luzula albida,* is content with somewhat drier and more acid locations. Both these species belong to the rushes, *Juncaceae.* With improved methods of forest management and the preference given to natural regeneration in relatively small areas, the forest weeds which used to be widespread in clearings have lost a great deal of importance. But they still play an important part wherever clear-cutting continues to be practiced. Flora which appears in clearings is often distinguished by wealth of color and by tall herbaceous plants. Particularly striking are the narrow-leaved willow herb, *Epilobium angustifolium,* forming large patches of magnificent red flowers at the peak of summer, the lesser burdock, *Arctium nemorosum,* with its huge leaves, and various ragwort *(Senecio)* species with large yellow flowers, Fuchs' ragwort, *Senecio fuchsii,* and wood groundsel, *Senecio silvaticus.* These first settlers in clearings are soon followed by shrubs which in turn prepare the way for the young forest trees–unless man by planting cuts short this natural development of vegetation known to the scientist as a succession. Among these forest pioneers are numerous species of brambles, *Rubus spec. div.,* sallow willow, *Salix caprea,* common elder, *Sambucus nigra,* weeping birch, *Betula pendula,* mountain ash, *Sorbus aucuparia,* and alder buckthorn, *Rhamnus frangula.*

In the fall all plants of the herbaceous layer appear to die. But although the leaves turn yellow, plant life is not in fact extinguished but usually withdraws into such underground shoots as tubers, bulbs or rhizomes which ensure survival during the cold season. A few species, however, are evergreen or at least survive the winter in a green state and are therefore particularly conspicuous among the bare trees; these include the above-mentioned ferns *Dryopteris lobata* and *Phyllitis scolopendrium,* as well as the ivy, *Hedera helix,* the lesser periwinkle, *Vinca minor,* species of wintergreen, *Pyrola spec.,* the *Anemone hepatica,* the hazel-wort, *Asarum europaeum,* and others. A similar process takes place in the earth's warmer climatic zones which have no winter but instead a pronounced dry season; to avoid desiccation the plants similarly withdraw into survival shoots and the many reserve substances contained in them enable these plants, with the arrival of the rainy season, to react with tempestuous growth so that, almost overnight, the dry steppes and bush forest are transformed into luxuriant vegetation with an incredible brilliance of flowers.

Shrub vegetation and climate

The shrub layer also protects the vulnerable forest soil. The forester is pleased to see numerous shrubs establish themselves under the canopy of the trees and cover the ground. With their annual leaf shed they ensure an appropriate circulation of nutritive substances in the soil; indeed their readily decaying leaves often have a catalytic effect on the tougher leaves of beech and oak, accelerating their chemical decomposition and reducing the formation of undesirable crude humus. Many shrub species are popular with deer for feeding and to rub their antlers on. This helps to reduce damage to trees in young stands. Quite apart from the fact that they also provide good nesting opportunities for the birds and shelter for animals, shrubs help to shelter young stands from the wind and thereby ensure favorable growing conditions. It has been proved that assimilation and hence wood formation is greater in a sheltered location than in a forest through which the wind can blow unimpeded. The silviculturist warmly welcomes the shrub vegetation and indeed tries to use the numerous available species to encourage growth at the forest edge, thus preventing the wind from entering the forest. Apart from the great ecological advantages it offers, such a forest edge is particularly delightful to see in the spring and the fall. It is magnificent at the time when sloe, *Prunus spinosa,* and white-thorn, *Crataegus spec.,* are in blossom alongside the guelderrose, *Viburnum opulus,* and wayfaring tree, *Viburnum lantana.* However the colors are even more brilliant in the fall. It is then not only the turning of the leaves but also the bright colors of fruits and berries which accomplish this regular annual miracle. The wild rose, *Rosa canina* and *Rosa pendulina,* bear their crimson hips on thorny shoots; the berries of the dogwood or cornel, *Cornus sanguinea,* and of the privet, *Ligustrum vulgare,* are brilliant black; and those of the spindle-tree, *Euonymus europaeus,* are a pastel pink or orange. The sour fruit of the sloe, dark blue with a whitish bloom, contrasts with the orange umbels of the rowan or mountain ash, *Sorbus aucuparia.* Squirrels search for the hazelnuts among the shrub's golden leaves. In the face of so much beauty one is prone to forget the nuisance of the thorns and spikes of these shrubs which obstruct access to the forest but at the same time protect the forest from various animals.

Forest fruits and poisonous berries

The great abundance of berries and fruits along the autumnal forest edge reminds us that man at one time largely depended on them for his food. Then, in the age of hunters and food gatherers, the fruits, berries and nuts of the forest, together with fungi and venison, probably accounted for the main part of his diet. Today berry collecting by the urban population is a largely recreational but no longer indispensable activity; at one time it was a matter of life and death. Any conceivable product, so long as it was not poisonous, was collected and either eaten at once or preserved by drying for the long winter. Civilized man today obtains from the forest only certain particularly tasty fruits and berries; the most popular are the wild strawberry, *Fragaria vesca,* the raspberry, *Rubus vitis-idaea,* the bramble or blackberry, *Rubus spec. div.,* and the cowberry and bilberry, *Vaccinium vitis-idaea* and *Vaccinium myrtillus.* People also pick the berries of the common elder and the scarlet-berried elder, *Sambucus nigra* and *Sambucus racemosa;* the rose-hip is still used for tea and jam. But the once highly important fruits of the *Sorbus* species (the whitebeam tree, the mountain ash and the service tree) or of the wild apple and pear, *Pyrus malus* and *Pyrus communis,* as well as the sloe and whitethorn, *Prunus spinosa* and *Crataegus spec.,* are spurned.

Poisonous plants and berries have also played an important part in human thinking and action. They were used not only to brew poisonous potions but many of them served the preparation of medicines and aphrodisiacs. The deadly nightshade, *Atropa belladonna,* with its beautiful shiny black berries was widely used as a cosmetic preparation for the eyes even in classical antiquity; in the European forests it grows as a tall bush in clearings and newly cut areas. Consumption of the beautiful berries can be fatal, especially for children. Its seeds are propagated by birds who suffer no harm from feeding on these cherry-like fruits. Equally poisonous are the scarlet berry-like fruits of the paradise plant of spurge flax, *Daphne mezereum,* the shrub which, earlier than any other, is smothered in delicate pale purple flowers and which exudes a positively intoxicating perfume. Other common poison plants in our forest are the herb Paris, oneberry or truelove, *Paris quadrifolia,* the cuckoo-pint or lords and ladies, *Arum maculatum,* the ivy, *Hedera helix,* yellow and blue wolf's-bane (the latter also known as monk's-hood), *Aconitum lycoctonum* and *Aconitum napellus,* the bittersweet or woody nightshade, *Solanum dulcamara,* which has violet flowers and grows in wet locations, as well as the yellow and purple foxglove, *Digitalis lutea* and *Digitalis purpurea.*

After this account of certain aspects of Central European forests a word should be said about at least one significant structural difference in the composition of the tropical and sub-tropical rain forests. Although they, too, are divided into moss, herbaceous, shrub and tree layers they contain in addition an entirely characteristic epiphyte vegetation which in the high tree crowns can develop into veritable epi-phyte meadows. Epiphytes are plants which grow on other plants, mostly on trees; they are occasionally known as overplants. The tropical rain forest is by nature dark and therefore offers little opportunity of growth to light-seeking plants. Numerous varied plant species therefore establish themselves on stems and branches in humus-rich moss cushions which are kept permanently moist by the frequent precipita-tion and the prevailing warm humid micro-climate. In a rain forest in Uganda more than 100 epiphytic plant species were found, of which up to 45 were growing together on the same tree. Ferns and orchids, above all, are present in generous profusion in such vegetation. Among the epiphytes there are numerous parasites which use their host plant not only as a support but also for their nourishment. The lianas which, though rooted in the ground, climb up the trees all the way to their crowns and to the light for flowering and fructification, complete the familiar luxuriant image of the tropical rain forest. The vegetation of epiphytes and lianas has its unquestioned centre of gravity in the tropics. Towards the poles the number of species and incidence diminishes, until in the Far North all that is left is lichens and a few mosses living epiphytically. Only a few species of genuine lianas survive in our regions. Worth list-ing in Central Europe are ivy, *Hedera helix,* the wild clematis, also known as traveler's joy or old man's beard, *Clematis vitalba,* and the common honeysuckle or woodbine, *Lonicera periclymenum.* Mention must finally be made of the mistletoe, *Viscum album,* a native evergreen and epiphytically living parasite which finds a livelihood on a great variety of trees. Mistletoe infestation of the white fir, for instance, of-ten reaches an extent where the tree perishes. Mistletoe played an important role in superstition: it was sacred to Teutons and Celts because of its seemingly magical way of feeding and keeping alive.

114 Trees destroyed by forest fire, with watch tower for fire prevention, in Saskatchewan, Canada
115 Bush clearance by burning in Ceylon (Sri Lanka)

120 Impression of tree bark in molten lava
121 Hollow mould of a charred tree trunk in red-hot lava

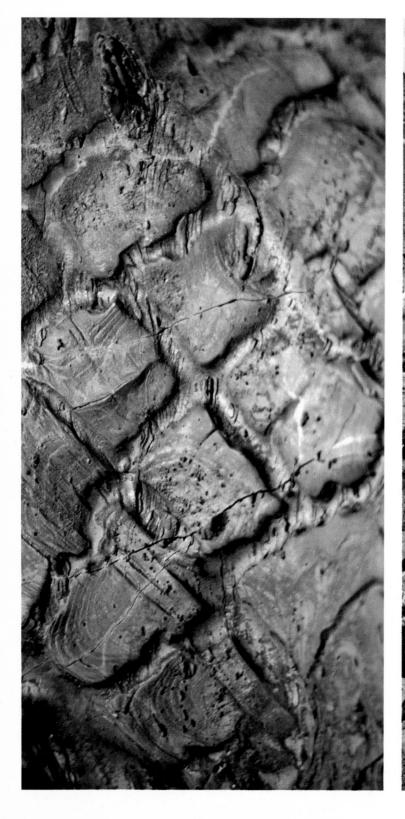

128 Umbrella-like acacias and common or blotched giraffes *(Giraffa camelopardalis)*, Africa

129 Zebras *(Equus quagga)* and elephants *(Loxodonta africana)* in the Amboseli Game Reserve

Destroyers of the Forest

Paul Bovey

Numerous animal species are temporarily or permanently attached to the living community of the forest, to its biocenosis. Many of them are of no importance to the trees, but there are a number of plant-feeding species which leads to the deterioration of the stands and to great losses whenever their numbers rise dramatically. The effect of these harmful animals in European forests has greatly increased since the turn of the 18th/19th centuries. It has been due to the introduction of new methods of cultivation which greatly altered the structure of formerly natural forests. In many regions, in order to achieve higher yields, the natural climax forests were replaced by artificial homogeneous stands; coniferous monocultures were planted in unsuitable locations and clear-cutting was practised on large areas. Man has thus contributed, however unintentionally, to the weakening of the resistance of the stands and promoted a fateful massive increase of insects in areas where previously they had been scarcely known or not known at all. Therefore the necessity arose to find means of preventing or controlling this development by intensive study of the pests and the factors governing their propagation. Since the last century special institutes have therefore been established and continually enlarged in all countries practising a modern forest management. Wherever forests are productively managed the need to protect them from their enemies is becoming more urgent, both because of the ever-growing threat and because of the increasing importance of the forests.

In the absence of accurate statistics, it is difficult to estimate the annual losses to European forests caused by animals, mainly insects. On the other hand, the research data of the forest organisations of North America provide an idea of the damages recorded. According to the 14th Forest Resource Report (1958) of the U.S. Forest Service, the «growth impact loss (tree mortality plus reduction of growth) resulting from insect attack in all forests of U.S.A. are estimated for an average year to about 3 billion cubic feet of timber. This amount is over 14 per cent of the net annual growth. The total annual mortality caused by insects was estimated to be over $1^3/_4$ billion cubic feet, or more than $1^1/_2$ times that caused by diseases and over 4 times that caused by fire.» «In Canada, the annual timber depletion caused by diseases and insects varied from 15 to 33 per cent of the amount of timber utilised by man during the past 30 years» (Anderson, 1960).

Importance of insects in the forest

Of all animals associated with the forest biocenosis the insects are economically by far the most important. They are represented by thousands of species, but many of these are not significant. Among phytophages (plant-eaters) these include the ones which feed on unimportant herbs or shrubs, or species living on trees but in number insignificant. Numerous insects are in fact useful to the forest, primarily the army of the entomophagous species (insect-eaters) which are constantly active as predators or parasites and greatly contribute to the maintenance of a biological balance among the phytophagous species. The useful species also include many inhabitants of the soil such as Collemboles (Springtails) and small beetles which, together with the Mites, play an important part in restoring organic substances to the soil, as well as the species decomposing the dead wood.

Harmful insects are all those whose activity reduces the forest's vitality in any form whatever. Different tree species exercise varying degrees of attraction for phytophagous insects. The oak as a broadleaved tree, the spruce, the fir and the pine as conifers harbor a rich insect fauna, while hornbeam and yew, for instance, have very few enemies. Any phytophagous species dependent on a specific plant for its nutrition must be regarded as a potential pest, becoming dangerous the moment it occurs in large numbers. Of all the insects living on a forest tree only a small fraction should be labeled as real pests. Their destructive character springs from the fact that, with the aid of their mandibles, they can consume parts of the plant or that they can suck up sap or cell fluids with their proboscis. Certain species, in both these groups, are distinguished by the formation of such typical galls that the agent can be identified from them with certainty. A stroll through a forest is sufficient for anyone interested in nature study to discover such formations on the most varied trees. Insects can also be active carriers of severe forest tree diseases.

Disregarding the polyphagous pests, which attack various plants indiscriminately, such as the Common and the Wood cockchafer, *Melolontha melolontha* and *Melolontha hippocastani,* or the Nun moth, *Lymantria monacha* whose greedy caterpillar consumes both the leaves of deciduous trees and the needles of conifers, most pests are selective with regard to their food-plant. The oligophagous species live and feed on several plants which generally are botanically related to each other, while the monophagous can develop only on one definite plant genus or one single species. Between the strictly monophagous and the polyphagous species there are all intermediate stages of oligophagy. Host specificity is linked to an insect's reaction pattern to olfactory, taste or visual stimuli emanating from the plant; these induce the female to deposit its eggs. Phytophagous insects frequently only consume certain parts of their host-plant. These specific characteristics make it possible to classify the forest pests under definite headings, such as «Leaf-eating insects or defoliators», «Inner-bark boring insects», «Wood-boring insects», etc.

In term of the physiological conditions of a plant at the moment of insect infestation we distinguish between the primary pests which attack healthy trees, and secondary pests which operate only on weakened trees with reduced or totally blocked sap flow. This distinction cannot always be made unambiguously and secondary pests may under certain circumstances become primary ones.

With the bark- and wood-destroyers, the most varied stages are found in this respect. Several bark beetles of the genus *Dendroctonus* in the coniferous forest of North America and the Poplar borers *Saperda charcharias* in Europe and *S.calcarata* in North America, for example, may be or are always primary pests. But the most bark beetles and the wood-boring insects are secondary in character. Only under special conditions, some species may become occasionnally primary. This applies particularly at the time of the mass propagation of the important bark beetle of the spruce in Europe, the *Ips typographus,* after pronounced drought or heavy hurricanes. Its populations multiplie rapidly under these conditions and the tentative borings of innumerable beetles into the healthy stems become so frequent that the trees are weakened and their occupation becomes possible. Other species settle only on more or less weakened or dead trees, or those felled some time before. Thus, the stages of decay of the trees are marked by successive species of bark- and wood-destroyers. Even worked timber is not spared by wood-boring insects. Among these the most importants are the Old house borer, *Hylotrupes bajulus* and the Furniture or death-watch beetles, *Anobium sp.,* in the temperate zone and the numerous Termites or White-Ants in the tropics.

From a practical point of view the forester distinguishes between physiologically and technologically harmful insects. The first category includes all species which threaten the health of the plant or weaken its vitality in any way; the second includes those which reduce the industrial quality and hence the market value of the wood. Certain species which attack healthy trees and penetrate into the wood belong to both categories.

Populations dynamic of forest insects

The harmfulness of phytophagous insects is closely connected with their population density, which varies both in time and local incidence. The study of these fluctuations is one of the main tasks of the forest entomologist. He discovers their causes and this enables him to prevent potentially harmful insects from crossing the harmfullness threshold. If this objective cannot be achieved, then population explosions can at least be predicted and counter-measures taken in good time.

Insect population density is the result of the interaction of two opposing groups of factors–its multiplication potential and acting against it, the environmental resistance. The fecondity of forest insects is generally great. According to species, a female can lay up to several hundred eggs. Assuming a low figure of 100 eggs per female the progeny of one pair, without opposing environmental resistance, would reach

625 million at the end of the 5th generation and that of two parthenogenetic individuals, such as aphids, the astronomical figure of 20 billion. Considering that most aphids produce more than five generations per year the result–as an American professor estimated for the White cabbage aphid–would be an annual progeny weighting 822 billion tons. This may be an extreme case, but all phytophagous insects of the forest would be capable of producing populations which would be bound to result in the rapid destruction of a stand.

Most of the potential forest pests cause real damage only over a short period, sporadically or periodically, and only in a part of their territory. Persistent pests, very common in agriculture, are rare in the forest. The fact that numerous potential forest pests do not multiply excessively either continuously or over long periods of time is solely due to the reason that over 95 per cent of the progeny of each generation perishes. A perfect equilibrium presupposes in theory an intracyclic mortality of over 98–99 per cent. Mortality from the egg to the imago stage is due to environmental factors of abiotic and of biotic character. Abiotic characters are such as climatic factors, temperature and humidity, as well as soil conditions. They determine the potential distribution area of the phytophagous species and entail a more or less high mortality of the various developmental phases. Within this framework the biotic forces act either as factors stimulating development with the food available, or as limiting factors through the action of natural enemies, diseases and intra- or interspecific food competition. The effectiveness of these limiting factors is the greater when the network of this inter-relations is denser. Experience shows that the stability of insect populations increases as the ecosystem, or the totality of living organism within a given environment and that of effective physical factors, become more complex. That is why the varied biocenosis of tropical and sub-tropical natural forests are rarely threatened by outbreaks of primary pests. For the same reason natural or artificial mixed forests in the temperate zone are as a rule far more resistant than homogeneous stands.

However the following example, quoted by F. Schneider (1936), shows that the balance in rich biocenosis, established over a long development, is nevertheless vulnerable. This concerns the liana *Uncaria gambir,* a native plant of Sumatra, which is being cultivated as a bush on cleared ground in large plantations for the production of tannin. While the moth species *Oreta carnea,* which lives on this liana, represent no danger to it in its natural habitat because of its slight population, its numbers began to increase more and more on the plantation the further away they were from the forest. This increase was solely due to the fact that its parasites have not followed the moth to the plantations–in particular the Chalcid wasp *Brachymeria euploeae,* which did not find the necessary blossoms there to supply it with nectar and pollen. In this species-specific complex of inter-relations it **was** enough to eliminate one link for a non-pest species to become a pest which makes it necessary for the plantations to be preventively treated every year again.

Happenings were similar in the temperate zone when in the last century foresters, disregarding the laws of nature, had artificial and equal-age stands (Fig. 36) planted outside their natural distribution area. This far-reaching change in the forest biocenosis resulted in a dynamic development of numerous forest insects, on a scale never before observed in the natural forests of the same regions. It is no accident that during the dry period of 1945 to 1949 a population explosion occurred of the Eight-spined bark beetle (book-printer), *Ips typographus,* especially in the homogeneous spruce stands of southern Germany, where thousands of acres of forests were destroyed. During the same time, the Curved-spined fir bark beetle *Pityokteines curvidens,* has almost partially wiped out the white fir outside of its natural area in the lower regions of the southern part of the Jura chain, while the fir stands of the Alps and of the Pre-Alps, as well as the natural mixed beech and fir forest of the Jura, have suffered no damage. It is often striking that an outbreak of leaf-eating insects causes greater damages in homogeneous stands than in mixed forests. In homogeneous stands, and even more so in equal-age forests, the insects are favored by plentiful food and relieved of the trouble of seeking out their correct food-plant. The reduction in the number of useful animals, above all of parasites, many species of which depend for their survival on intermediate hosts, upset the balance of the biocenosis. Besides, what matters is not merely the assortment of food plants but the variety and multiplicity of the flora generally. Our earlier example showed that a plant which provides food as flowers for pest parasites may exercise a decisive influence on the development of an insect.

The variation in the resistance of forest types to insect attack must induce the forester to create or maintain a biological balance unfavorable to the pest. Such tasks demand time, and frequently a mass outbreak can be nipped in the bud only by direct intervention. Counter-measures presuppose accurate knowledge of the pests, of the kind of damage they cause and of their life-cycle. Before looking at the means available to us for forest protection it might be as well to cast a glance first at the most active groups of forest insects.

Leaf-eating insects

A particularly rich fauna of insects inhabits the crown of the forest trees, where they attack buds, leaves, shoots, flowers and fruits. Although fruit or seed-eating insects may limit the natural chances of seed production, the most dangerous pests are among the leaf-eaters or defoliators. They are principally butterflies, moths and sawflies whose larvae, caterpillars or loopers, may if present in massive numbers, destroy the foliage of whole stands. A major part in this is played by *Macrolepidoptera* and *Microlepidoptera* species.

A few Macrolepidoptera species occur sporadically or periodically in European forests. One of the commonest is the Nun moth, *Lymantria monacha,* of the Lymantriidae family, whose polyphagous caterpillars indiscriminately attack broadleaves and conifers. Extensive damage is caused by them on non-needle-changing conifers at the beginning of the vegetation period. Extensive tall spruce forests are at particular risk, especially if monoculture has resulted in large homogeneous areas. German, Scandinavian and Russian forests, as well as those of the Danube region, have been repeatedly devastated. The weakening of the trees caused by the destruction of their needles gave rise to prerequisites for the attack of bark-breeding bark beetles, causing rapid tree death. In broadleaves and larches among the conifers, which regenerate their foliage after being stripped, the damage is usually confined to loss of growth. The Gypsy moth, *Lymantria dispar,* is a pest of mainly broadleaves forests in various parts of Central Europe. It is also an enemy of the evergreen and cork oaks of Spain, Corsica and North Africa. Some time before 1870, it was introduced into the U.S.A. where it spread in the East. The destruction it caused was at first catastrophic and is still important. In the great plains of Central and Northern Europe, the pine forests are frequently attacked by caterpillars of some monophagous *Macrolepidoptera,* such as the Bordered white beauty, *Bupalus piniarius,* the Pine beauty *Panolis flammea,* and the Pine lappet *Dendrolimus pini.* The outbreaks of these pests can continue over several years and, unless counter-measures are taken, must lead to the death of the stands owing to secondary attack by bark beetles and certain weevils. The outbreak of *Panolis flammea* between 1922 and 1924 engulfed 1,250,000 acres (500,000 ha) in northern Germany, resulting the cutting of 706 million cubic feet (20 million cubic meters) of dry timber; the losses amounted to over 224 million dollars (700,000 million DM). In southern Europe and in Asia Minor, the pine forests are attacked by the Pine processionary moths, *Thaumetopoea pityocampa* and *T. wilkinsoni.* Their caterpillars live in extensive nests of webbing from where they set out in processions to forage at night. In the event of mass outbreaks all the needles can be stripped with disastrous results. An increase of these insects is moreover very unpleasant for the forest personal and for the tourists because the caterpillars are equipped with readily detached urticating hairs.

Among the important Macrolepidoptera in North American forests, beside the European Gypsy moth, there are more native species which are also harmful for the trees, such as the Hemlock loopers *(Lambdina fiscellaria lugubrosa* and *L.f.fiscellaria)* as most destructive pests of the western and eastern forests of conifers, the Forest tent caterpillar, *Malacosoma distria,* as pest of hardwoods, and many others. In the case of heavy infestations the Forest tent caterpillars reduce the production of maple syrup, and the migrating larvae could create inconveniences to recreationists.

Among the vicious defoliators of European and North American forests are several *Microlepidoptera* which cause a great deal of damage in spite of the small size of their caterpillars. One of the most interesting species is the Larch bud moth, *Zeiraphera diniana,* whose outbreaks in the alpine larchwoods above 4,250 feets (1,300 m) occurs periodically in intervals of eight to ten years. It causes a characteristic browning of the stands during two or three consecutive years. The larch produces new needles in August. As a rule, the trees do not die but suffer a loss of wood growth, a reduction in cone production, and hence in seed formation. In the alpine valleys, moreover, the aesthetic aspect of this damage is very conspicuous. The Silver fir bud moth, *Choristoneura murinana,* just as *Zeiraphera rufimitrana,* can occasionnally occur in large numbers on white fir in various forests of Europe. In the Northern U.S.A. and in Southern Canada, a relation of it is the notorious Spruce bud worm, *Choristoneura fumiferana,* which is one of the outstanding defoliators of North America, on various conifers, mainly the Balsam- and the Douglas firs. After complete defoliation, the conifers are attacked by secondary insects, such as Bark beetles, and the trees will be killed. Several outbreaks have occured in the spruce-fir forests of this region and its population explosion in Eastern Canada during the ten years period 1910–1920 caused the death of a quantity of timber amounting to virtually the Canadian total available of commercial timber. The devastation was repeated on a no less alarming scale between 1945 and 1959 and necessitated the employment of aircraft over vast areas. In Europe, oak coppices and oak forests are attacked by the Oak leaf-roller, *Tortrix viridana,* whose caterpillars strip the leaves in spring. This is a dangerous pest capable of sustending itself over the years in varying strengths and one of the causes of the depression of oaks. Apart from butterflies and moths, the sawflies are of importance in coniferous forests although their larvae usually show outbreaks in small areas. Two of the most injurious species in Europe are the Spruce sawfly, *Pristophora abietina,* and the Pine sawfly *Diprion pini.* A large number of sawflies are noxious in the coniferous forests of North America. The most are indigenous as several *Neodiprion* sp. on pines, but five species are introduced from Europe: *Pristophora erichsoni* on the larch, *Diprion (Gilpinia) hercyniae* on spruces, *Neodiprion sertifer, Diprion similis* and *Diprion frutetorum* on pines.

Among the leaf-eaters of the forest mention should be made of several beetles which can occur in large numbers especially on broadleaves. These include the strictly monophagous Elm leaf-beetle, *Galerucella luteola,* which chiefly attacks ornamental trees in Europe and North America, and the Large poplar leaf beetle, *Melasoma populi,* in Europe.

In addition to the biting species there are many sap-sucking insects inhabiting the crowns of our forest trees, mostly *Heteroptera* or *Homoptera,* represented by bugs, leafhoppers, aphids and scale insects. The damage caused by them is not comparable with that of the leaf eaters and only a few species are of economic importance in silviculture. Among these are primarily the aphids of the *Chermesidae* or *Adelgidae* family which are strictly confined to conifers. Their development follows an often complicated cycle with a switch from a primary host (spruce) to a secondary host (larch or fir or pine). Young spruces not infrequently show large quantities of galls of the European species *Chermes viridis* and *Chermes strobilobius,* this last introduced in North America. From these galls hatched winged migrating forms which continue their cycle on larches. Per contra, the two related paracyclic species *Chermes abietis* and *Chermes tardus* have lost their capacity of migration and live continuously on the spruce with a simple cycle of two parthenogenetic generations. *Chermes abietis* was also introduced in North America early in the nineteenth century. The white fir in Europe harbors the most dangerous pest *Dreyfusia nordmannianae* *(= D. nüsslini)* which was brought from the Caucasus. Its larvae deform the needles of the new shoots. In its native land this species lives on two hosts–the Oriental spruce *Picea orientalis* and the Nordmann's fir *Abies nordmanniana*. Because of the absence of the primary host in the forests of Western Europe it remains on the White fir, as secondary host, exclusively in parthenogenetic forms. The related paracyclic species *Dreyfusia piceae,* the Fir bark louse or Balsam wooly aphid, attacks in Europe the stems of the White fir now and then so intensively that they look silvery white. Having been introduced in North America it attacks various species of fir, principally the Balsam fir, which proved more vulnerable. Thus while this pest is of scarcely any importance in European forests, where it is moreover decimated by a rich predator fauna, it soon became a dangerous pest in Canadian forests.

Among sap-suckers mention should also be made of the *Thysanoptera* or Thrips–minute insects which suck the sap in the parenchyma cells with their short proboscis. The Larch thrips, *Taeniothrips laricivorus,* whose first attacks were observed in Czechoslovakia in 1926, has spread through all forests of continental Europe wherever larches occur. The worst affected are young trees since puncture by larvae and imagos causes malformation of the terminal shoots.

Bark and wood-boring insects

The stems and branches of many forest trees harbor numerous pests which, apart a few Hymenoptera and Termites, mostly belong to the beetles. Several species are able to attack healthy trees, but most of them are secondary pests. Some of those which attack weakened trees are no less dangerous since they can bring about the ruin in a short time even of trees which in normal circumstances could recover. This is true in particular of the bark-breeding bark beetles which are multiplying in disastrous manner in the coniferous forests.

According to the location of the damage the insects of the stems and of the branches are divided into two main groups–those infesting the bark and developing in or under the bark in the bast, also the phloem insects, and the wood borers proper whose development takes place entirely in the wood itself. Few species, especially some *Cerambycidae* or Long-horned borers, such as the Sawyers (*Monochamus* sp.) start their development under the bark and complete it in the wood.

The most widespread and most injurious inhabitants of the bark belong to the *Scolytidae* family and they are the bark beetles. They should not to be confused with the *Bostrychidae* or Large Powder-post beetles, another family of wood-boring beetles which live chiefly in the tropics. The bark beetles are small insects with cylindrical body 1–9 mm in length. Some of them settle on broadleaved trees but most of them are hosted by conifers. There are more than a hundred species in the European forests and just as many in North America. The luxuriant tropical and sub-tropical forests harbor hundreds of species, some of them not yet described. There they occur especially on felled, dying or dead trees.

The oligophagous or strictly monophagous bark-breeding bark beetles have a most interesting life cycle. For propagation their imagos are attracted to favorable breeding trees. In polygamous species, the male starts its boring activity on its own by providing a «nuptial chamber» in the bark. Between two and five females are then attracted into this chamber. After copulation, each of these females bores an egg gallery from this nuptial chamber and deposits its eggs in small lateral niches. In the monogamous species the female begins the burrow and does all or nearly all the construction work. As soon as the larvae are hatched they start boring separate larval galleries which get steadily wider, terminating in a pupation chambre. After hatching and a period of intensive feeding the beetles leave this chamber through a circular hole to winter in the ground or to establish a new generation. A complete tunnel system therefore consists of one or more egg galleries and numerous larval galleries. Each species thus has a definite and often typical gallery-pattern which allows its agent to be readily identified without examination of the insect. Figure 130 shows the gallery-system of *Ips typographus* under the bark of the Norway spruce, a pattern familiar to every European forester.

The vulnerability of the trees is closely connected with the osmotic pressure of the sap. The most dangerous bark beetles can attack trees when the pressure is only slightly reduced by drought or by damages from leaf-eaters. In Europe, the following forest bark beetles inhabit conifers: the Eight-spined bark beetle (book-printer) *Ips typographus,* the Six-spined spruce engraver *Pityogenes chalcographus,* the European four-eyed spruce bark beetle *Polygraphus polygraphus* on the spruce; the Curved-spined fir bark beetle *Pityokteines curvidens* and its relations *P. spinidens* and *P. vorontzovi* on the white fir; the Twelve-spined fir bark beetle *Ips sexdentatus,* the Six-spined pine bark beetle *Ips acuminatus,* and the two *Blastophagus piniperda* and *B. minor* on pines; *Ips cembrae* on larch. On elm trees, the Larger and the Smaller European elm engravers, *Scolytus scolytus* and *S. multistriatus,* the late introduced in North America in about 1930, are very noxius. They play the main role in spreading a serious disease caused by the fungus *Ceratocystis ulmi* which leads to the elimination of this tree species. First identified in Holland in 1919, this disease has become a scourge throughout Europe and North America causing the death of many thousands of trees, chiefly in avenues and parks. The fungus which develops in twigs, branches and in the stem, prepares the ground for the attack of the bark beetles which promote the infection of new branches and the rapid spread of the disease. The young imagos in the galleries get infected with the fungus spores which adhere to the surface of the insect or find their way into the intestinal canal. The new hatched beetles move on to young healthy twigs for their maturing feed, where they bite the bark and thus spread the disease which furthers the mass propagation of the *Scolytus*–a real vicious circle. The same part is played by the American species *Ips grandicollis* in the spreading of blue strain, a fungus disease affecting pines.

In the great forests of North America where overmature stands are frequent, the bark beetles play a very important economic role. They are responsible for about 90 per cent of the total losses due to insects. The most harmful are the *Dendroctonus* bark beetles which are represented by about twenty species infesting the bark of coniferous trees. Some of these beetles are always typically secondary, others can attack healthy or lightly weakened trees. The most important species of this genus are the Southern pine beetle *D. frontalis,* the Northern spruce beetle *D. obesus,* the Northern pine beetle *D. ponderosae* and the Western pine-beetle *D. brevicomis.* In Europe, this genus is only represented by *D. micans* which is particularly noxious on spruces in Central Germany, Belgium and, until 1940, in new stands of Sitka spruce in Holland, Denmark and Schleswig-Holstein.

Several engravers as the Californian five-spined engraver *Ips confusus* in the western forests, the Oregon pine engraver *Ips pini (= I. oregoni)* in the western and boreal forests, the Southern pine engraver *Ips grandicollis* in the eastern forests from South Canada to Florida, and several others, if not so aggressive as the *Dendroctonus* and secondary in character, may be very noxious after drought or hurricanes.

Recent researches conducted by two groups of American workers, one of the University of California and the Standford Research Institute, headed by D. Wood and R. M. Silverstein, the other of the Boyce

Thompson Institute for Plant Research under the direction of J. P. Vité, contributed largely to a better understanding of the aggregation of bark beetles on selected trees. The pioneer-beetles, males of polygamous species such as *Ips,* females of monogamous species such as *Dendroctonus,* are first attracted by odors of the host trees. But at the beginning of the boring, or soon after, very attractive substances or pheromones, concentrated in the hindgut of the pioneer-beetles and released by defaecation, diffuse into the air. These pheromones, acting at very low concentration with host terpenes, determine the mass aggregation of beetles of the same species on logs infested by the pioneer individuals. Therefore they are named «aggregating pheromones». The pheromones of three species of *Dendroctonus* and one species of *Ips* were isolated, identified and synthetized. Their presence was detected, but not yet identified, in other species in North America and Europe. This important discovery allowed us to explain why the control method of bark beetles with «trap trees» gave good results in the past.

The bark-breeding beetles in small numbers are always present in the forests, forming what foresters call an «iron reserve». As soon as favorable conditions occur for their multiplication in a large area, for instance through drought or defoliation from primary leaf pests, their numbers increase with enormous rapidity and in most cases the destruction caused by them can assume massive proportions, leaving foresters powerless.

The Pissodes of the Weevil family or *Curculionidae* are closely related to the *Scolytidae.* They differ from the bark beetles in the fact that only the larvae bore galleries under the bark. They start where the female deposits its eggs on the surface of the stem or of a branch. These species are exclusive to conifers. Under the bark, related to both these groups, are the representatives of two further families, the *Cerambycidae* or Long-horned borers, characterized by long antennae, and the *Buprestidae* or Metallic beetles with their striking colors.

The bark-breeding long-horned wood borers do not have the same economic importance as the bark beetles. Some of them nevertheless can do a lot of physiological damage by attacking healthy or slightly weakened trees, such as the *Tetropium* species which attacks conifers. The beautiful Sawyers of the genus *Monochamus* which occurs on the stems of conifers in the forests of Europe and North America, cause not only physiological but also technical damages in that their larvae penetrate deep in the wood for pupation. Among the Metallic wood-boring beetles, only few species need be regarded as pests of temperate forests. The most dangerous one in Europe is *Agrilus viridis* which can cause serious trouble in beech-woods weakened by drought. The southern and equatorial forests harbour a large number of species of this family.

In addition to the bark-breeding species, there are many which penetrate direct into the wood and both start and end their development there. They can cause physiological and technical damage or purely technical damage according to whether they attack living or dead trees. The wood-boring bark beetles or *Ambrosia* beetles are of particular interest. They breed *Ambrosia* fungi by infecting their galleries with spores which are transferred by the imago from one generation to the next. The larvae feed on the coating of conidia which lines the egg galleries. The development of the larvae requires a continuous cleaning of the galleries by the parents, including the removal of larval excrements. Male and female remain with their progeny until they are adult. These are probably the first beginnings of the social relationships. Fresh coniferous logs in Europe and North America are frequently ruined by the Striped Ambrosia beetle, *Trypodendron lineatum,* and broadleaved logs in Europe by *Trypodendron domesticum* and *T.signatum* whose galleries penetrate deep into the sapwood. The Columbian timber beetle, *Corthylus columbianus* is one of the most aggressive species of American Ambrosia beetles. It enters in the stems of hardwood living trees and there bred successfully. The trees are not killed, but the burrows remain in the wood as permanent defect.

In the tropics, the wood-boring bark beetles are joined by numerous representatives of a related family, the *Platypodidae* or Flat-footed Ambrosia beetles. In the absence of very dangerous primary pests, they are among the most destructive enemies of felled logs in the tropical regions. Two species occur in Europe and half a dozen in North America, which attack felled logs of hardwood or conifers.

Among the Long-horned wood borers, the Great oak longhorn, *Cerambyx cerdo,* is one of the most attractive (Fig. 131). Widespread in European oak stands it seeks out old, damaged or weakened trees. The period of development is two years. As the wide larval galleries go right in the heartwood, they diminish the commercial value of the logs. Some years ago, in the Rhineland, weakened stands by change of the watertable were so heavily infested that the massive oak stems were riddled with the holes bored by this beautiful beetle. Poplar plantations often fall victim to the Poplar borers of the genus *Saperda* which develop as primary pests in stems and thick branches of healthy trees. Several large beetle species confine themselves to trees already in a state of decomposition, such as the elegant Stag-beetle, *Lucanus cervus* (Fig 145). This species favours oak forests occupying warm positions where the adults could be observed flying at twilight. Conifers felled in the late summer are visited by large yellow, blue or brown wood-wasps or Horntails of the hymenopterous family *Siricidae* whose females deposit their eggs in the wood using a long ovipositor. The larvae develop in the course of two to three years so that the imagos may hatch even from timber already processed.

Protection of the forest

As we had seen, there have always been forest insects even though they were less important in the past than they are today. The greater injuriousness of insects, due to the development of silviculture, is closely connected with the establishment of artificial stands, frequently outside their natural range, with certain management methods, and with the introduction of foreign pests. The most recent experience teaches that the main task of forestry consists in strengthening the natural resistance of forests against pests. This requires an accurate knowledge of the biology and ecology of the pests and a complete understanding of the healthy forests. Restoration of an upset balance is a long-term task which can only be solved if due account is taken of natural laws. Silvicultural methods are increasingly based on the latest finding of plant sociology and are concerned with a transformation of homogeneous stands. The choice of trees is to make on the strength of edaphic and climatic requirements. In many regions of Europe, mixed forests are gradually replacing homogeneous spruce stands planted during the last century. Clear-cutting is increasingly replaced by the methods of successive and selective cutting which make greater allowance for the biotic balance of the stands.

However, the mistakes of the past cannot be rectified from one day to the next. There is every reason to hope that the devastation caused by pests will be reduced in the future. But we cannot expect ever to exterminate these scourges of the forest completely. Although mixed forests are less vulnerable they are not entirely safe from attack. Whatever the composition of the forest, the timber, once out, must always be protected against secondary wood-boring insects. Effective as preventive measures may be, forestry management must be in a continuous stage of alert to move against menacing pests. They must spot the beginning of outbreaks at an early stage since this, according to a forest entomologist, is winning «half of the battle». The methods used can be mechanical, chemical or biological.

Mechanical methods have largely been abandoned today. The only exception is the use of «trap trees» which continues to prove useful in the extermination of local outbreaks of bark beetles. The method consists in first removing the infected trees and then felling healthy ones on which the imagos have settled. Before their progeny can develop fully these trap trees are debarked over a cloth and the bark burnt. If practised in proper time, this method makes it possible to check the beginning of local outbreaks of many secondary bark beetles in the coniferous forests.

After the discovery of the synthetic organic insecticides, chemical means of insect control became more and more important and DDT was the forest insecticide «par excellence». It was applied with success, together whith other chlorinated hydrocarbons (Aldrin, Dieldrin) and with organophosphates against the most dangerous forest insects, as for instance the most important defoliators and certain soil insect pests, and also for the protection of the wood. After the discovery of these weapons most of the pest control problems appeared to be solved. However, three main disadvantages resulted from their generalized and often irrational use: the selection of resistant strains of pests, the disruption of the natural balance and the cumulation of residues of chlorinated hydrocarbons in the fat bodies of animals and man, residues which persist through food chains. These disadvantages led North America and several European countries to the ban of chlorinated hydrocarbon insecticides and at the same time to an increased interest in biological methods of control, including the use of natural enemies and of entomopathogens.

Beneficial insects are able to re-establish the original natural balance in areas where exotic pests have been introduced. U.S.A. and the British Commonwealth have world-wide organizations for the study and the collection of natural enemies in their native area and for their introduction in the new areas where their hosts have become a pest. Natural enemies are often mass reared in insectaries before their release in a new area. Indigenous entomophagous insects, parasites and predators, have also been used for the control of agricultural pests, to a lesser extent in forestry. However, several forest defoliators can be mass reared today on artificial media, thus creating the basis for the mass production of parasites and predators to be released in forests. Viruses and bacteria, and especially the well known *Bacillus thuringiensis,* have been utilized against forest insects as sawflies (viruses) and caterpillars (viruses and bacillus). Although biocontrol methods are very interesting and do not create unnecessary environmental problems, their use appears rather limited. It is therefore necessary to look for other methods of control. During the last ten years efforts have been made to find out new techniques for the control of pests without contamination of the environment. Intensive research has been developed along three main lines: (a) the sterile male technique, i.e. the release of males of the target species which have been sterilized by radiations or by chemosterilants; (b) the use of sex-pheromones or aggregating pheromones which have recently been isolated from some forest lepidoptera and bark beetles, and chemically defined; (c) the use of plant derivatives or of synthetic substances which have on insects a similar action as juvenile hormone and inhibit the metamorphosis in certain species.

These three fields of research offer some hope for the future, but are still in an experimental phase. For the protection of the forests we have to rely in the meantime on chemical insecticides, if possible more specific and less dangerous for the environment. However, with the present state of knowledge and the means at our disposal, the forester must profit from all the natural forces active within the forest and interfere with chemical means only where this is absolutely indispensable. Forestry will have to be guided by the principles of integrated pest control, which combines the advantageous features of both chemical and biological control methods with a good protection of the useful species, parasites and predators. Among these the birds and the red forest ants deserve our particular solicitude.

It is to be hoped that the forestry-entomological research now being conducted throughout the world for protecting the forests of the temperate zone will be vigorously persued and that the experiences will be profitably utilized in the increasingly exploited tropical forests.

141 Reindeer *(Rangifer tarandus)* in a larch forest of the
    Yakutian taiga

142 Male red deer *(Cervus elaphus canadensis)*

148 Doe and kid of big-eared deer *(Odocoileus hemionus)*, native to Western Canada and U.S.A.

149 Natural camouflage of the adder *(Vipera berus)* among
oak leaves

The Forest in the Past

Alfons Meyer

The history of mankind is closely linked with forest and trees. Even without getting entangled in controversial ideas on geological and prehistoric antiquity it is difficult enough to know how to interpret certain sources. Such sources are very scarce, unreliable and often misleading: "Howl, O ye oaks of Bashan!" we read in Zechariah around 590 B.C. Are we to conclude from this exclamation that the landscape in question was then covered with trees which the translation of the original biblical text calls "oaks"? To this day, and in all countries, there has been a great deal of confusion in the names of different trees and this has made reliable interpretation of documents impossible. When, how and for what purpose were those ancient forests cut? Certain passages in Luke and Matthew state that the grass standing in the field today will be cast into the furnace tomorrow. From these sentences the forest historian Seidensticker concludes that in Palestine, formerly rich in forests, men had to resort to the burning of dry grass in areas where wood was beginning to be in short supply. Some of us may not agree with this interpretation. To quote another example, Seidensticker, to whom we owe a comprehensive history of the forest in antiquity, believes that the burning of the Carthaginian fleet by the Romans proves that the latter had sufficient stocks of building timber in their own country. A more obvious conclusion, to our mind, would be that they simply wanted to destroy the naval vessels of the enemy. In point of fact, we learn from the Roman author Quintius Ennius that during the First Punic War (264–241 B.C.) the Romans were trying out various species of timber to determine their suitability for naval construction. Pine, cypress, ash and ilex were all used, but chiefly the great oaks *(magnae quercus)* were utilized.

Forest and wood in tradition and language

Historical records of human origin are very recent considering nature's immense span of time and space. In Central Europe the earliest records are the laws of the Germanic peoples who inhabited Helvetia. About the year 500 King Gundobad issued the Burgundian Book of Laws. In it is a ban on the cutting of fruit-bearing trees *(arbores fructiferas)* in forests not personally owned. The ban covered mainly oak, but also beech, Spanish chestnut, and wild fruit trees; in a less severe form the ban also applied to "*pinis et abietibus*", i.e. pine and white fir. The "Pactus Alamannorum" of the seventh century, which codifies the laws of the Alamanic population of what is now Switzerland, in spite of its mass of detail on other questions, contains very little information on the forest cover beyond the fact that oaks were plentiful. The Western Gothic Book of Laws of the Merovingian period mentions a tax payable for the right to use acorns for livestock fattening. The term "forest" first occurs in 556 in a deed of the Merovingian King Childiberth. The Franconian kings imposed an interdiction on many extensive forest areas *(foreste)* reserving all rights for themselves, especially those of hunting, fishing and collecting forage for livestock (i.e. acorns and beech masts), as well as the privilege of bee-keeping, most important in the Middle Ages, involving as it did the production of honey and candlewax. *Foresta* became more frequent as feudal lords, bishops, dukes and court officials interdicted particular forests, reserving them for their own hunting and, either through gifts or long-term use, acquiring them as their private property. In these *foresta* the subjects were forbidden, on pain of severe punishment, to hunt, fish or collect forage, honey or wood. From *Neustria* the *foresta* also spread to Burgundy and *Austrasia* east of the Rhine, and generally throughout the territory of Franconian rule which under the Carolingians eventually embraced the major part of Europe. The term *foresta* occurs repeatedly in the famous *Capitulare* of Charlemagne of 813. It says there, among other things: "De forestiis, ut forestarii bene illas defendant, simul custodiant bestias et pisces." Thus the task of foresters at the time was, above all, the protection of hunted game and fish. It is significant that in France the term "Eaux et Forêts" has survived for forestry. The forest ran counter to the original Germanic legal concept of common ownership of woodland and grazing land. The earliest occurrence of the German word "Wald" ("wood") is in a text by the translator Notker in the monastery of St. Gallen; he even adds a very early nature observation by saying that the sun lends the wood a golden tint. Notker lived about the year 1000. Around 1100 a German commentary on Genesis was compiled in the Styrian monastery of Vorau; among God's blessings is listed the fact that "He gave the wood its beauty". About that time various versions of the Nibelung epic took shape: in them we find frequent mention of woods, including the passage, interesting to the historian of the chase, which refers to the stalking of wild boar, bear and bison. The medieval German poet Walther von der Vogelweide frequently mentions the woods, sometimes in connection with a pure spring. In a poem written by another author in 1229 we read: "To a rich wood it matters little if a man loads himself with timber."

There are even older occasional references in Roman and Greek authors. But the forest is an elastic concept. What to the Southerner seemed a primeval forest with enormous trees may have looked rather more modest to Celtic and Germanic eyes. Thus Tacitus's description of the Teutoburg Forest, where the Roman legions under Varus suffered such a disastrous defeat in 9 A.D., strikes us as rather exaggerating its terrors. Consider Pliny's account of the acorn-bearing trees in the Lusitanian Sea and in the Zuiderzee, whose branches were so thickly entangled in soil and water that the Roman fleet could not maneuver. And Ammianus Marcellinus in 367 speaks of a Swiss frontier desert, a "*desertum*" and of horrendous forests along Lake Constance: *"horrore silvarum inaccessum lacum"*. Nevertheless, in the course of the first four centuries A.D., Helvetia was developed as an outer bulwark of Roman rule against German invasions. In the area of the great highways and camps the forest had to be extensively cleared. From Geneva and Martigny important roads, both for military purposes and trade, ran to the magnificent capital of Aventicum and thence via Petinesca near Biel, Solodurum, and Ultinum to the large camp of Vindonissa near Brugg and as far as Turicum and Ad Fines (Pfyn), where the road from Rhaetia also ended. Seneca, the unsuccessful tutor of the Emperor Nero, in a letter describes the forest of his time: "Step into a grove filled with ancient trees of exceptional height; the branches, one above another, and the dense foliage block the view of the sky. This tall growth of the forest, the mysterious silence, the eeriness of the deep unbroken shadow arouse in you a belief in the deity." Another excellent observer was the poet Virgil to whom we owe not only the Aeneid but also the Georgics, the book of agriculture. In it, in Book II, we read about the oak: "Therefore neither gale nor foul weather nor pouring rain can topple it; it stands unshaken and in endurance surpasses many generations of grandchildren and many unrolling ages." Now and again we find references to the forest in Ovid–in connection with the Metamorphosis of Erisichthon there is an account of the felling of a huge oak of 15 ells (56 feet) circumference, "a giant of the primeval world, a forest in itself, from which hung ribbons and votive tablets"–i.e. an ancient votary tree. According to Herodotus, the Persian King Xerxes made a gift of golden ornaments to a huge plane tree in Asia Minor; the gold was hung on its branches and a member of the King's suite was appointed its permanent guard and custodian. Under the Roman Emperor Tiberius massive larch logs were hauled to Rome from the Rhaetian Alps for bridge construction. Larches were considered water- and fire-proof.

Germanic love of forests and gods suffered a cruel blow when in 724 Winfried, known as the Monk Boniface, laid his axe on the ancient sacred Donar oak at Giesmar in Hesse in the hope of wiping out veneration of the Germanic thunder god. In spite of the warning of a hurricane the tree eventually crashed to the ground and nothing happened; no lightning hurled by Donar struck the impious axeman. This historically attested Donar or Thor oak reminds us of the mythological concept of the worldash Yggdrasil, a symbol of the world. Three massive roots bore that tree–one reaching towards Nifelheim, the realm of the dead, the second reaching towards Jötunheim, the land of the giants, and the third spreading towards Midgard, where mortal men lived. This was the place of the Urdh spring by which sat three grave silent women–the Norns of the past, the present and the future. They spun the threads of destiny of the newborn–few silken or golden threads but many threads of sack-cloth, with one thread of suffering and death. They watered the world ash with sacred water to ensure that it would live and produce leaves. Yet the tree was beset by dangers: a goat was nibbling its leaves, stags fed on its shoots and buds, which then were lost as the hours and days of the seasons, and as the years of eternity. And down below, from Helheim, the dragon Nidhögg was rearing; together with other serpents it gnawed the roots. In the treetops an eagle had its nest; between it and the serpents down below the squirrel Ratatöskr scuttled up and down, carrying discord and bad news. Attempts have been made to prove that this worldash was more likely a worldlinden. However, we cannot go into these mythological interpretations, interesting though they are, for an understanding of the forests in distant antiquity. We will confine ourselves to one more brief reference–the ancient Greek legend of the serpent near Lerna which grew two new heads for every head cut off. This legend no doubt symbolically represents the continuous struggle which the early inhabitants of the swampy region of Lerna hat to wage against the morass: as soon as one hole was blocked the swamp and bog would overflow at two new spots. Only Hercules, by strength and cunning, succeeded eventually in slaying the serpent with a hundred heads–or, as we would say today, in redeeming the land.

Determining the age of prehistoric timber

Prior to World War I scholars tried to establish the former distribution of wood species by an examination of topographical names (toponomasty); in Switzerland such work was done by, among others, Brandstetter in Lucerne and Escher-Bürkli in Zürich. They found that of 4,198 names 3,573 applied to broadleaves and only 625 applied to conifers – one of the many proofs of a very much wider distribution of oak and beech in antiquity. For Germany, Austria and Switzerland, Edmund von Berg has listed 6,053 local names referring to broadleaves as against only 852 referring to conifers. Similar results were obtained by Neuweiler in his examination of prehistoric timbers from lake dwellings and Roman camps. Shortly after 1900 some black oakwood was raised from the Rhine, from the bridge built by Caesar, and processed into expensive furniture as "German ebony". In the Steller Moor near Hanover, Conwentz discovered an entire submerged yew forest. Jens Holmboe proved the presence of massive oak stems in the moors of the Norwegian skerries. Similar finds of oak have been made in coastal waters off Cornwall so that some scholars now consider it proved that at the time of the King Arthur and Tristan legends some islands in the Irish-Cornish Sea were linked and covered with oak forests. A Moscow engineer, Maleyev, in a report submitted in 1935 stated that attempts were then being made to raise sunken oak trunks from rivers in order to meet the requirements of the Russian timber industry. These discovered resources are estimated at scores of millions of cubic feet. Ancient tree stumps and the belt of alpine rhododendron in the Alps testify to the former tree line which, as early as the Middle Ages, dropped by 600 to 1300 feet in many regions. In the Far North the tundra has also gained ground: in Finnish Lapland, Renvall established the presence of large numbers of tree stumps on the Utsjoki River.

Another important method for forest history is the counting of growth rings. Thus the "Annual Growth Ring Chronology of Oaks in the Spessart", investigated by B. Huber in 1949, made it possible to date certain buildings in Bavarian Franconia. From stem sections of Californian sequoias the American scientists Douglas, Ellsworth, Huntington and Antews proved in 1911 that Pueblo Bonito, for instance, was built in 919, using trees which were then 219 years old; this Indian city flourished in 1067 and was certainly inhabited until 1127. The climatic character of these regions was traced back into antiquity and confirmed by comparison with droughts during historically attested periods. After countless investigations these foresters and archaeologists exclaimed in admiration, "Trees do not lie!". Sections of tree trunks disclosed more of the original inhabitants of California and Arizona than any humans did. These Californian giant sequoias provide much food for thought. They were young seedlings when Moses led his people out of Egypt and the Pharaoh's hosts vanished in the Red Sea. They had long been mature when the legendary duels between David and Goliath and between Achilles and Hector were fought. The whole of Greek and Roman history unrolled while on the other side of the world the tall tops of these giant trees were towering like church spires into the pure air. The oldest living thing in Europe was probably a yew cut near Brabourne in Kent, in southeastern England, with nearly three thousand growth rings. Switzerland has to content itself with a nearly 1000-year-old yew on the Hasenmatte slope in the Solothurn Jura.

Another kind of forest history "archive" is provided by pollen analysis, first developed in Sweden about 1930. The delicate pollen from the pistils of the male flowers, each typical of its tree species, is scattered by the wind; if it falls into moors or peat bogs it may survive tens of thousands of years. Its post-glacial layers indicate first an immigration of steppe plants and *Dryas* flora, followed by a birch period, followed in turn by pine and hazel; eventually, in the neolithic age, roughly between 3000 and 1800 B.C., the mixed oak forests become dominant. There followed an immigration of beech and maple; in the bronze age, until about 850 B.C., the fir predominated; the iron age (Hallstatt, La Tène) until the birth of Christ saw the spread of the spruce; and the subsequent Roman period saw the appearance of Spanish chestnut, vine and fruit trees.

The centuries between stone age and bronze age witnessed the erection of lake dwellings. Traces of domestic animals, fruit and berries have been found. For the past two decades, however, reference to "lake dwellings" has had to be made with some caution, for Oskar Paret, a Stuttgart archaeologist, has tried

264

to disprove as untenable the whole idea of lake dwellings first formulated by Ferdinand Keller. Paret maintains that all settlement was exclusively on dry land. These new ideas were first challenged by Keller-Tarnuzzer in 1948. Paret, for his part, was supported by Professor Vogt, who was in turn opposed by Laur-Belart, with Lüdi in between the conflicting views. The problem has not yet been solved.

An entirely new method for the determination of the age of wood samples was developed by the American professor of chemistry, Willard Frank Libby. His "radiocarbon dating" examines materials for their content of carbon atoms of atomic weight 14. The timber is carbonized and the C-14 content established. Libby made his first experiments with wood samples from a giant sequoia stem whose date of felling was known, and with others dating back to ancient Egypt; the historically attested periods proved the reliability of the C-14 method.

Another novel method for the determination of former wood species and forests was developed by the Swedish geologist, de Geer. It was further improved by Nipkow of Zürich. This is based on annual layers of deposits both in Southern Sweden and in the mud of Lake Zürich. In conjunction with pollen analysis, Max Welten, by his drillings in the dried-up Faulenseemoos near Spiez, has since been able to establish a picture of the forest history from the late ice age to the present day. According to Welten's strata count the period from 3200 B.C. to the present, i.e. a time span of roughly 5000 years, has been a period of beech.

Let us try, with the aid of all the above-mentioned aids, to obtain a picture of the forest in the past. For Central Europe this seems relatively easy.

Forest clearance for human settlement and forest interdiction

We have mentioned the age of the great migration and the first laws touching upon the forest. At that time the need for forest clearance was still overriding. Clearance became a task for the monasteries: the monastery of St. Maurice was founded in 516, St. Gallen und Disentis in 614, Romainmôtier about 640, Einsiedeln in 838, Bevaix in 998, and Engelberg in 1120. Mostly, they were deliberately located in thick forest and in remote regions since the heavy labor of forest clearance was an express monastic injunction: *ora et labora*. The other monastic injunction, that of poverty, soon yielded to an accumulation of property. The monasteries rapidly acquired rich possessions, largely through donations and legacies. Whenever forests are mentioned in ancient deeds they almost invariably occur in the form of a legacy: "Ad salutem animae patris" money and land, forest, vineyards and fields were bequeathed, especially just before the expected end of the world in 1000. When Judgement Day did not come, there was a sudden explosion of a hunger for life. From about 900 onwards the founding of churches and villages developed rapidly. The period of major clearances was completed about 1300 in the plateau regions and in the mountains along important passes. We need only refer to Urseren (on the Gotthard) and to the fully cleared Rütli alm (Lucerne), completed about 1290. Nearly all present-day settlements existed at that time, although of course the villages were far less populous than today. Nevertheless, wood consumption was greater because it was almost exclusively used for houses, bridges, wine presses and implements, and because there was as yet no substitute for its lavish use for heating. The forest of the Swiss Mittelland was predominantly mixed deciduous forest; a widespread type was underwood, i.e. wood growing on clearings which was cut and utilized in very short rotation. The distribution of forest, arable land and grazing was by then stabilized. The forest had been forced back to the territory where to date it has rarely been challenged.

The oak, then still very plentiful, was regarded as an agricultural fruit-bearing tree which, in open grazing forests, reached right up to the edge of the towns and was found in hedges or individually in almost every field. Its fruit, the acorns, were indispensable for fattening pigs which were then universally kept, even in the towns. The best hams grew on oaks, as Simplicius expressed it during the Thirty Years War. Only the introduction of the potato, from about 1760 onwards, brought about a change in public attitude to the oak: acorns had become superfluous. From a fruit tree it became an ordinary forest tree now cut, mostly too young, for the sake of its excellent timber, whereas previously, in order to obtain a lot of acorns, it had been allowed to grow excessively old. The second disaster for the oak occurred 100 years later with the construction of the railway when the oak woods were used up in many places for the production of cross-ties.

For the scholar it is a rare treat to discover, among thousands of deeds covering the period from 750 to 1705, a rare one which allows conclusions to be drawn concerning the forest, its species of timber or its management. A few examples will show the kind of information provided.

The so-called Testament of Queen Bertha goes back to 962; among the gifts connected with the foundation of the monastery of Payerne it mentions, alongside two other pieces of woodland, "una quarum fagifera altera glandifera", the first record, therefore, of beech and oak woods in what is today the Canton of Vaud. Dating back to 1306 we have a "Sentence arbitrale" from the Archiv de Torrenté in Sion, according to which the most important species of wood in the central Valais were "daylles, sappins, laries, warnyos", i.e. pine, spruce, larch and fir. From a family quarrel between the Countess Isabella von Neuenburg with her stepmother Marguerithe de Vufflens we discover that the latter, in 1378 in the forest of Boudry, "avait fait couper deux mille chênes et plus et autres arbres portant fruit, ayant par ce moyen ruiné la forêt".

This clearance and forest destruction was opposed at an early date by sporadic protection of forests. In 1323 Chamoson limited grazing; in 1339 Muotatal placed its forest below the Flühen under interdict; in 1387 Altdorf did the same for its forest, made famous by Schiller's "William Tell", where the trees bleed when an axe is laid on them; in 1397 the then still extensive forests in the Urseren Valley were put under interdict, but, as a result of traffic over the Gotthard, Furka and Oberalp, they largely disappeared even before the fighting between French and Russians. In 1480 Hans Waldmann prohibited the felling of oaks in the Zürich area; in 1488 the city of Berne prohibited all further forest clearing; an interdiction decree is known also from Adelboden, another was issued in the Turtmann Valley in 1515; in 1644 the rural district of Davos protected its forest in the Zügen; in 1577 the tapping of larches was prohibited in the Valais.

Diagnosis is one thing and cure is another. In spite of all regulations and often hair-raising threats the reduction and deterioration of forests continued inexorably. Wood offenses were not regarded by the people as theft. As long as they saw forests about them their wood was squandered. Frequently a couple of pines would be cut down to make a pair of wooden clogs; for the sake of a small twig with Arolla pine kernels a tree would be cut down and left lying. The worst destruction was caused by mines and glassworks. Grossmann summed up their effect on the forest in the words: "What the ironworks have left behind is a bare country denuded of forests."

As for research into the history of forests, the most extensive work, apart from Switzerland, has been done in Germany. Among major studies mention should be made of Hausrath, von Berg, Roth, Schwappach, Dengler, Endres, Hilf, Mantel, Hornstein and Hesmer. Switzerland still lacks an overall study, especially as there are very considerable variations among the 25 cantons and often among districts and municipalities. But there has been some detailed work on individual regions and specific problems–by Weisz, Grossman, Combe, Hagen, Hauser and Meyer. On France there is the forest history by Huffel, and on Belgium that by Goblet d'Alviella. For most other countries the sources do not go back far enough; as a rule they start only when forest destruction became conspicuous, resulting in karstification, steppe formation and disturbances in the supply of water.

As for species, the forest picture in Europe has remained the same for the past few thousand years. True, a number of promising species have been imported, chiefly from North America, but only few of them have proved successful. Even Weymouth pine, Douglas fir and acacia have not significantly changed the appearance of forests. But human interference has changed the picture considerably. Broadleaved forest has yielded to coniferous forest. The spruce mania in the 19th century forced back the oak and beech; it established itself in areas formerly growing larches. Some changes resulted from rivalry between species. Unbridled utilization and forest clearance were followed by centuries of conflict with agriculture and grazing. About 1200 the "Colmar Chronicle" complained that there were too many forests in Alsace, "making the land infertile for grain and wine". There were numerous trees over ten feet thick. Eventually, in spite of all political fluctuations, a biological compromise had to be reached, a reconciliation between forestry, agriculture and viticulture. Then, about the middle of the 19th century, a young forestry science developed almost abruptly. In connection with a physiocratic assessment of agriculture and forestry and a fear of a timber shortage a groping developed for a scientific basis for the treatment, regeneration and blending of forests. Not until our century did forestry research create an understanding of the nature of forests together with the opportunity of deriving lasting and maximum advantage.

Countries with a marked decline in forests

Our sources from classical antiquity refer to extensive magnificent forests in all the countries of the Mediterranean area which, after all, were then "the world". The mountains from the Syrian Lebanon and the Anatolian Dagh to the Sierras of Andalusia and the Rif of Morocco were well covered with trees. All these mountains have long been denuded. And together with the forests, famous granaries have disappeared in historical times; St. Augustin still saw a hundred-fold grain yield in the area of Carthage, now a desert. It used to be customary to attribute the disappearance of the forests to climatic changes or even to Persian armies, Punic fleets or vandal invasions. A much more likely hypothesis is that, ever since the days of the "divine swineherd" Eumaius, goats and sheep have gradually destroyed the original forests and rendered impossible their regeneration. All endeavors everywhere were invariably aimed at extending pastureland; protection, let alone maintenance, of the forest is a very new idea. As recently as 1857 we have a record from the Eifisch Valley in the Valais: "Nous voulons faire une montagne de génisses au lieu d'une forêt." Similarly a rare "Codice veneziano del 1600", with numerous naive colored pictures, drastically describes the consequences of deforestation, attributing it to desiccation of springs and to inundations, as well as to forest fires allegedly caused by shepherds: "Ecco la prima e principal ragione del Male, ecco il fuoco, che per far pascoli e Campi doppo il 1500 ogn' Anno più uolte se appiccia..." Clearly Venice realized about 1600 what effects deforestation could have. Venice, as a great power in the Mediteranean, required countless trees for its powerful navy and these could be obtained only from the mountains of Dalmatia. Even the construction of the city in the lagoons demanded hundreds of thousands of durable oak piles. The Venetians even tried to cultivate the curved timbers they needed for their ships and gondolas.

The present owners of those hillsides have described these Venetian attempts in a sumptuous volume published by the Yugoslav Forestry Administration which contains pictures of some of these strangely curved timbers. Many trees were systematically trained into abnormal growth to make the hamstrung stems provide timber for oars, rowlocks, back supports or blades. The fleet built from those forests helped establish the glory of Venice but the Dalmatian mountains were turned into arid karst, a term that has become synonymous with denuded, desiccated, hard and perforated rocky ground where forests can never grow again. Trieste, too, is much to be blamed. At the beginning of the 16th century this city had handed over its forests to its citizens for their free use and this resulted in the extermination of every single tree; indeed such was the hunger for wood that even the roots were grubbed up. Frequently entire forests were burnt rather than allowed to fall into the hands of the Venetians. Even the severest penalties never deterred forest offenders anywhere; about 1740 the Emperor Charles VI forbade the lopping of trees, hay-making and all grazing in the Austrian territory of Dalmatia and imposed the death penalty for setting fire to forests. In Albania the once vast forests have likewise been destroyed. Unrestricted cutting of timber totally upset the water budget; fierce torrents came into being with the disappearance of the rain-retaining forests, causing inundations and turning fertile land into swamps. Where once extended profitable forests and cultivated fields, all that is left today is impenetrable scrub or fever-infested swamps. Especially rich pine and oak forests also existed on the island of Korcula, where Venice had transferred its naval arsenal and where the local hardwoods were used to build three-deck galleys with three banks of oars.

Cyprus, too, has its forest story. According to Eratosthenes the island was originally densely covered with forests. The Pharaohs of Egypt and the Phoenicians worked them ruthlessly, cutting timber for shipbuilding and mines. Under Alexander the Great the exploitation was continued. However, a decline in the population and a century of peace were enough to enable the forest to spread once more, even into fields and orchards. Strabo reports that, in order to check this excessive spread of the forest each Cypriot was granted the ownership of as much soil as he cleared of trees. This law proved effective. When mines were first established and new demands made on shipbuilding (between 1489 and 1571 the Venetians also used Cyprus timber for their fleet) the island was totally denuded. The forest disappeared altogether. What Strabo could not have foreseen was that, following the island's depopulation through numerous wars, the bare hills would once more produce a natural forest cover; but this was stripped once more, this time by goats. These alternations continued until the exhaustion of the soil put a halt to them. Building timber continued to be exported into modern times, in fact until the British occupied the island in 1878. In 1873 the Turkish Government had commissioned a French forestry expert to submit an opinion on the island's forests.

Reference should be made in this connection to an island elsewhere—St. Helena, perhaps the clearest illustration of the effect of uncontrolled grazing. In 1502 goats were introduced to the island and multiplied rapidly. The island's dense forest survived for another two centuries, but then the old trees began to die and, since there was no regeneration, the forest disappeared suddenly. Its place was taken by grassland. When the tragic fact was understood, an extermination of the goats was begun in 1730; but by then it was too late to save the forest.

An account of the forest between the Black Sea, the Bosphorus and the Sea of Marmara by Fikret Vural (Ankara, 1940) states that it had already disappeared as early as Byzantine times. Professor Schimitschek's book proves that extensive territories along the Turkish shore of the Black Sea were totally deforested. Disastrous karstification can be seen on the hill near Kastamoni.

Corsica remained the best-wooded island in the Mediterranean. It is strange that in Roman times the edible chestnut was not found there; it was introduced much later but soon became such an exclusive source of popular nourishment that the French, after capturing the island, were only able to break the stubborn resistance of the Corsicans by destroying their chestnut groves. Mallorca and the Pityusae islands (now Ibiza and Formentera) have almost entirely lost the forests in which, according to Plutarch, the Roman general Sertorius found refuge. Crete exported timber to Egypt as early as 2000 B.C.; the flourishing civilization of its ancient capital Knossos was hostile to the forest. As recently as 1921 Chief Forest Inspector Hess saw large quantities of charcoal being loaded on ships there. The few surviving forests are no longer sufficient; many regions have no other fuel left but the roots of a few olive trees and shrubs degenerated into macchia. Hess predicted that the cypress would also soon be extinct. What has gone on being destroyed over thousands of years will scarcely be saved by a belated reforestation program. In 1932 Constantin Regel wrote: "Grazing or agriculture has destroyed the vegetation [of Crete] to such an extent that no traces of it have survived.".

Gaul, according to ancient accounts, was so densely wooded that squirrels were said to be able to jump from tree to tree in an unbroken forest from Toulouse all the way to Normandy. Caesar refers to the dense forests in many regions. According to the Gallo-Roman poet Ausonius there were areas with extensive oak woods, while along the western coast vast stretches of land were covered with pinaster pine. The endless wars and migrations of people caused forest devastations which were largely responsible for the silting up of ports such as Aigues-Mortes. The sand dunes began to advance irresistibly. In 1887 the first steps were taken to stabilize them. Laborious reforestation with Scotch pine has regained considerable areas for cultivation; however, the now customary resin production does not make for healthy forest growth. Moreover, the forest is time and again threatened by fire. The saying current in the Gironde: "Qui a pin a pain" has every justification. Over vast areas of southern France grazing, especially by enormous flocks of sheep, has destroyed the forest and rendered its regeneration impossible. "Transhumance", the trek of the flocks, has long been a major danger. Small wonder that goats and sheep are known there as "rasoirs à quatre pattes". In the Cevennes one can travel for days through bare stony desert and only a few ancient lichen-covered beeches and scattered pines on remote hillsides testify to the fact that once these "causses" were well-wooded, even though the only things growing in this depressing landscape nowadays are thistles.

Goat grazing has also contributed to the denudation of Spain over the centuries. Only a Don Quixote would fight hopelessly against goats and sheep. True enough, Barbey, a native of the Vaud, remarks in his monograph on the near-extinct Pinsapo firs of Andalusia that the small wandering and climbing "usines laitières" were indispensable to the population and that there were means of preserving both forest and grazing. In the Serrania di Ronda it is reported that, right up to their exhaustion, the Pinsapo forests had provided timber for the "invincible" but storm-wrecked armada. Only small remnants of the once vast forests have survived here and there as nature reservations. The book "Las Estepas de Espana y su vegetación" by Eduardo Reyes Prosper, published in Madrid in 1915, contains terrifying accounts of the vast extent of steppeland. E. Furrer reports that, according to local sources, Aragon had once been predominantly forest land. All that survives now are stunted junipers fragrant with resin; a few rare survivors of Aleppo pine and ilex have also escaped extinction.

A glance across the Mediterranean reveals a very marked decline in Algerian forests. According to Lefèbvre nearly 2,224,000 acres of forest, about half the forests of the Tell Atlas, were burnt between 1875 and 1897. French colonization forced the Arabs back into the still well-wooded mountains, where they let their sheep and goats graze and often caused fires, either through negligence or deliberately. The German zoologist Franz Kollmannsperger, in his book "Threatening Desert", written after an international Sahara expedition in 1953–54, has given an impressive account of how forest destruction and soil degeneration come about. The areas of bare rock resulting from forest destruction and soil erosion become nuclei of progressive devastation, just as a focus of infection spreads in a body which lacks natural resistance. The result of this development is the "man-made desert". Researchers such as the Frenchman Lavaudan and the German Heske confirm that the present-day forest of North Africa is merely a small remnant of once vast forests. These forests extended far to the South as proved by survivors of the *Acacia tortilis* in Southern Tunisia, the occurrence of the *Pistacia atlantica* in the steppes of the Northern Sahara, and the remnants of woodland in Central Saharan regions. Former woodlands have been swallowed up by desert.

According to Hartig, South Africa must be described as another classical land of forest destruction. Thus, for example, the Widdringtonia forests, at one time the characteristic forest type of the South African west coast, have been all but destroyed by cutting, over-use and fires.

In nearly every country the forest has deteriorated. Even in the U.S.A. ruthless destruction has been turning the seemingly inexhaustible forests first into prairie and increasingly into steppe and desert. Byrd wrote in 1685: "The water is clear and delicious, the river rolls down as a crystal stream of very sweet water." This water has long been dark brown and undrinkable. According to Gut of Zürich, nearly 300 million acres had been ruined by soil erosion in the U.S.A. by 1941. About 300 years ago 820 million acres, or 50 per cent of the surface, were still under a dense forest cover. Now the forest has shrunk to 25 per cent of its original area. Huge dunes cover the much-vaunted prairie. Pasture is so poor in places that sheep and rabbits no longer find any food. Large desert gaps yawn amidst the most fertile part of the U.S.A.: the soil has gone with the wind. Hugh Potter Baker in a thesis published in 1911 has compiled numerous testimonies by American and German scholars on the origin of the prairie; we mention only one, by Thompson in 1883: "Far out in the plains tree stumps and charred wood can be dug up, proving that once there was forest." James Fenimore Cooper's famous novel "The Last of the Mohicans" and his other "Leather Stocking Tales" describe magnificent forests with a hundred species of wood. According to Dr. Köstler, professor of silviculture at Munich University, the U.S.A. between 1780 and 1930, i.e. in 150 years, cleared 346 million acres of forest, European Russia about 74 million acres in the 19th century, and Rumania 2.5 million acres between 1920 and 1930 alone—as much as Switzerland's total forest area. Small wonder that SOS messages nowadays addressed to Washington and the various State Governments—are interpreted no longer as "Save our souls" but as "Save our soil".

The forests of the past cannot be restored, nor does anyone wish to do so. But today's forests must be protected. By means of ever more sophisticated reasoning, care and management, modern forestry science tries to compensate in quality for what has in many countries been lost in quantity. As long ago as 1790, when Georg Ludwig Hartig first ventured to draw up forestry management plans for 120 years ahead, such planning was enthusiastically welcomed by Friedrich Schiller, whose son became a chief forester. Until then he had always seen foresters as huntsmen and killers of wildlife. But now he exclaimed: "You are great men: you work in anonymity, without reward, free from the tyranny of selfishness, and the fruits of your devotion will ripen for a distant posterity."

Spruce cones, of *Picea abies*, with 300 seeds

154 Woodcock *(Scolopax rusticola)*
155 Cuckoo *(Cuculus canorus)*

156 Jay *(Garrulus glandarius)*
157 Great spotted woodpecker *(Dendrocopos major)*

158 Vigilant fox cub *(Vulpes vulpes)*
159 North American raccoon *(Procyon lotor)*

160 Badger *(Meles meles)*, a peaceful beast of prey
161 Roe kid *(Capreolus capreolus)*, sensing danger

165 Common maple *(Acer campestre)*, young growth

166 Hummingbird hovering by the brush-like flower of *Carthamus tinctorius*
167 Passion flower *(Passiflora edulis)*

168 Vanilla blossom *(Vanilla planifolia)*
169 Passion flower *(Passiflora quadrangularis)*
170 *Heliconia bihai* with hummingbird ▷

The Forest at Present
and in the Future

Peter Grünig

The tasks assigned to the modern forest are exceedingly varied and extensive–but surprisingly enough it is possible to meet them all. However, their realization depends on a crucial condition–forests must cover sufficiently large areas, in evenly distributed and extensively linked complexes. The forest is expected to meet simultaneously all the following demands: it must produce good quality timber, healthy water and clean air; it must ensure habitability and amenity for the land; and it must sustain and promote man's mental and physical well-being.

The forest in jeopardy

Everywhere–in highly developed areas as much as in developing countries–the forest is in extreme jeopardy. There is no lack of drastic examples. In the tropical developing countries, for instance, thousands of acres of the most luxuriant primeval rain forests are cleared each year to provide virgin soil for agriculture. But since these rather fertile soils are neither properly worked after clearance nor adquately fertilized, they are exhausted within a few years, no longer used, and gradually abandoned. Instead, new forest land, which seems to be abundant, is cleared and the impoverished soil is left to its fate. Sometimes wood will grow on it again at some later date, but as a rule these are thinly stocked secondary forests, lacking economically important species and scarcely able to discharge their protective functions. In consequence their soil is frequently eroded. Who has not seen those bare rain-ruined and infertile hillsides in tropical and sub-tropical regions, hillsides formerly covered by dense forest in whose shelter man felt secure and whose fields, if correctly worked, produced consistently high yields? This kind of forest clearance may temporarily assuage the first hunger in over-populated regions of certain developing countries but it is not a long-term solution of the problem because the destruction of the forest also wrecks the production basis of agriculture. It is a well known fact, repeatedly confirmed by history, that the destruction of forests makes poor nations even poorer.

Over the last few decades forest destruction has assumed alarming dimensions in Central Europe, even though the forest is no longer available on the same plentiful scale as in the past. The wave of forest clearance which continued into the Middle Ages largely shaped the present distribution of settlement, agricultural land and forest–a distribution which is harmonious even though not deliberately planned. Our present-day landscape has developed through history and has, over the centuries, stood the practical test of balance. It is therefore dangerous, rash, and indeed irresponsible to tamper with such a harmoniously structured landscape. But what in fact is happening to forests in an over-populated Europe?

Building land is scarce and forest land cheap; so the forest is cleared, if possible close to the cities. The population increase and our higher standard of living demand new communications. Where are these most easily built? Through the forest–hence the forest is sacrificed. Where is there land left for large modern airports? In the forest, of course–hence forest destruction. Motoring and flying demand fuel, which means the building of refineries. Where are these best located? In the forest–therefore more forest clearance. Where are the many new industrial plants needed for a further expansion of the economy to be located? Again in the forest. What is more, all this construction requires gravel, stones and cement. Where are these materials to be found? Beneath the forest; to clear the trees, therefore, is a matter of course. The population explosion is accompanied by a rapidly rising flood of refuse and trash. Where is it to be dumped? Needless to say, on cleared forest land.

It is both depressing and alarming to see forests being used and misused in this way. It is no exaggeration to state that we are in the middle of a clearance wave similar to that of the Middle Ages. But whereas forest clearance then was a vital necessity, it is nowadays merely an easy choice for which, unless a halt is called to this trend, we shall one day have to pay dearly. There can be no doubt that the forest has become the minimal factor in the European landscape. Through human stupidity and inadequacy its future is seriously threatened. But this means that all our other ecological foundations are similarly imperiled. Is our generation to remain passive in the face of this dangerous development? Are we to watch our landscape being impoverished and eventually made derelict? Are we to watch what today is still a habitable land being turned into man-made steppe or civilization-made desert? Anyone who thinks this view exaggerated should consider the Ruhr. There, as a result of forest destruction, conditions have already been brought about which are intolerable. Forests in the Ruhr have become a rarity, and those which have not been swallowed up by industrial plants or cities are threatened by the unbelievable pollution of the air. Conifers perish without exception. If anyone is looking for recreation in the sparse and largely sick forests he had better not stroll from highways or tracks, for after the first few steps he will be smothered in soot and dust which has been deposited as a black coating on the leaves of trees and shrubs and also on the ground vegetation. Is this the landscape, the country, we want to leave to future generations?

Forest-mindedness and forest policy

What then is to be done to halt this trend? It is not easy to find a satisfactory answer to this question. To begin with, it is vital that people recognize the spiritual and material value of the forest, that they remember what they owe to the forest. We do not wish to repeat here what has already been said elsewhere in this book. But we do want to emphasize that man cannot live without the forest. This realization has, over the centuries, given rise among many people to what we might call forest-mindedness. By this we mean an understanding and love of the forest, the conviction that the forest is our most reliable friend and no longer the terrifying enemy it used to be. Unfortunately, this sympathetic attitude toward the forest only exists among a minority of the population and has not yet become a universal attitude. Until it does it will be exceedingly difficult to pursue an active, constructive, or militant forest policy. The first basic prerequisite, therefore, is the establishment of a universally and deeply rooted pro-forest attitude; this demands extensive educational and public relations effort.

In the past most forest experts concentrated entirely on the economic aspect of the forest and were reluctant to take their purely technical problems to the public. Now, however, they are compelled by circumstances to abandon their reserve and to ensure for the forest the place which it must occupy if our landscape is to stay healthy. The forest is no longer a hobby of a few idealistic forest lovers but a problem of concern to the population as a whole, i.e. a factor of political importance.

Positive support for the forest, a deep-rooted conviction of the forest's spiritual and material value–these are indispensable prerequisites of a modern and militant forest policy, one that will be reflected in appropriate forestry legislation. Most forestry laws today confine themselves to a purely defensive attitude. Because its existence was accepted as a matter of course and because it seemed scarcely threatened, there was frequently no reason for enshrining an active forest policy in appropriate legislation. But in the face of increasing demands which are universally being made on the forest, and also because the forest is increasingly becoming an object of profiteering and thereby being decimated, this defensive attitude must be abandoned. An active forest policy can be pursued only as part and parcel of overall regional planning. As a dominant landscape element the forest merits priority treatment by this modern branch of human settlement policy. That is why forest lovers should be members of appropriate planning bodies. So long as the forest is treated as a stepchild there is a danger that, slowly but surely, it will disappear from metropolitan areas although it is there that it has to perform its most vital functions as a refuge and recreational area for the population. Forest land near cities should therefore not merely be preserved as a health-giving spring but indeed enlarged; there can never be too much forest in densely populated regions.

City forests and the welfare function

The German city of Frankfurt am Main may be regarded as a model of an active forest policy. Here 750,000 inhabitants have at their disposal some 12,350 acres for recreation, for their water supply, and for the regeneration of their air. By decree of the city administration the forest has been declared a natural reservation and its sale prohibited. It thus enjoys complete protection although elsewhere in the Federal Republic of Germany the forests are not protected by law. Whereas the Frankfurt city forest was visited by a thousand people a day prior to World War II, it is nowadays visited, in fine weather, by more than 40,000 people in search of recreation. Yet in spite of the large number of visitors it is being managed on an economic basis, except that timber production is regarded as less important than water yield. Thus in 1962, 14 billion U.S. gallons were withdrawn from its groundwater as drinking water–a quantity to be considerably increased in the future by way of artificial groundwater enrichment with water from the Main River. By its progressive forest policy–rooted in the exemplary support given to the forest by the population of this metropolis–Frankfurt has set an example of how a purposeful inclusion of the forest in regional planning makes for a successful combination of its commercial, protective and social functions. Frankfurt, moreover, is not an isolated instance. The forests in the neighborhoods of Cologne, Hanover, Munich and Stuttgart fulfill similar roles. What is obvious in the case of Frankfurt is that the successful forest policy pursued by the authorities is fully and unanimously supported by its total population; it is in fact the reflection of the public's pro-forest attitude

Extensive woodlands, especially near big cities, counteract the city dweller's progressive loss of individuality. In the forest, in God's free nature, he can be himself, unobserved by his neighbors. The realization that the forest retards a progressive loss of individuality should be fully taken into account in regional planning. There is a danger today that unbridled building will cause settlements hitherto separated by green belts to coalesce, giving rise to mammoth cities which no longer meet the inhabitants' vital needs and frequently challenge human dignity. The available settlement area should be increasingly interspersed with sufficiently large green areas. Thus, residential and industrial zones should be separated from each other by a green belt. These functions are discharged by existing forests and also by open spaces which might advantageously be forested in order to embed the satellite settlements in refreshing greenery. In this way it is possible to ensure that, in spite of a growing population and increasingly dense building, the townsman can still live in a location where he feels happy and where he is not instantly aware of living in the middle of a city. In the immediate neighborhood of his home, he will find opportunities for strolling, for recreation and for escape from the everyday hustle and bustle. Large-scale forest belts are moreover a boon in that, at no additional cost, they make a contribution to the purification of the air and the improvement of water supplies. Economic, protective and welfare functions are best fulfilled by well-tended forests with a plant composition as near natural as possible. In such stands the forester has the best chance of utilizing individual trees as each is ready for cutting and thereby achieving the highest possible yield without detracting from the forest's protective and welfare functions. Financial returns from forests have lately been declining; forest owners are more and more insistently calling for profits, and a danger therefore exists that short-sighted considerations may give rise to the establishment of forests designed solely for achieving the highest possible financial yield without discharging their other equally important tasks. Preference is still given to the spruce in many parts of Central Europe, in evident disregard of the disasters experienced with this economically valuable but ecologically rather dangerous species. Any relapse into the rigid forms of a 19th century land profit doctrine, oriented solely towards financial yield, would undoubtedly clash with the modern trend towards an active forest policy which alone can ensure our environmental foundations. The planting of equal-age spruce and other unnatural monocultures should therefore be discouraged and preference given to a consistently economical mixed forest, composed by species and structure as close to natural forests as possible; such a forest is just as aesthetically satisfying and profitable. Only such a forest will in the long run give valuable and lasting service to Man.

Although the forest still represents our earth's greatest wealth it is now seriously and variously threatened in its appearance and indeed in its survival. Let us therefore guard this wealth wherever we can: this is the best and most constructive protection of nature and homeland.

Care for the forest;
It is the surest source of prosperity.
Quickly devastated by the axe,
It only matures slowly.
All our deeds and actions
Will be judged by our grandchildren.
Let us be solicitous while there is time,
So that one day they may praise us!

Notes and Information on the Illustrations

1 Over the last few decades Britain has carried out extensive reforestation, chiefly with conifers. Even so, forests only account for 6 per cent of the country's area. That is why English parkland and forests, with their ancient oaks and beeches, enjoy particular protection and are lovingly cared for.

2 Finland, with 72 per cent of its area in forests, is the most heavily wooded country of Europe. Pine *(Pinus silvestris)* and spruce *(Picea abies)* account for three-quarters of the forest. At the same time, Finland has 60,000 lakes.

3 The turning of the summer-green leaves of beech and oak-woods in the fall is a particularly striking phenomenon. The name "beech" is believed to be derived from an ancient word "boko" meaning red. The change of color of the leaves in the fall is due to a recession of the green pigment chorophyll, leaving carotin, xanthophyll and other pigments to predominate in the leaf tissue.

4 Heavy snowfalls can cause considerable pressure and fracture damage in forests. Evergreen conifers such as pine and spruce are better fitted to resist snowstorms if they have narrow crowns and short branches, as in Scandinavia and at higher altitudes in the mountains.

5 Coastal redwoods *(Sequoia sempervirens)* in Prairie Creek, Redwoods State Park, in Northern California (41° North latitude) between the cities of Eureka and Redding in the Klamath Mountains. The Californian coastal range receives ample precipitation. The trees are over two thousand years old and more than 330 feet high.

6 Palm forest in Jamaica, in the Caribbean between the Equator and the Tropic of Cancer at 18° North latitude, located near Ocho Rios on the north central coast of the island. These are the long-fronded Royal palm *(Maximiliana regia)*. However, there are over 1,000 tropical palm species. They very rarely form extensive pure stands but instead grow singly or in small groups. Palms supply bread, wine, oil, wood, sago, palm butter, palm oil, and palm sugar.

7 Primeval bush in New Zealand (Fiordland National Park). Mixed *Podocarpus* broadleaf and *Nothofagus menziesii,* related to the European beech forests.

8 Extensive spruce forests of *Picea canadensis* or *Picea glauca* (white spruce) are found at the foot of Mount Healy in the interior of southern Alaska. Together with *Picea nigra* (black spruce or Canadian fir) and *Larix laricina* (tamarack) these species represent the northernmost boundary of the forest. The spruce is distributed from the Atlantic to Alaska. The wood is resinous and is used for paper manufacture and, because of its resonance, also for musical instruments.

9 Chugack Mountains in Alaska. In the foreground dwarf birch *(Betula glandulosa),* with primeval spruce *(Picea glauca)* in the sandy soil of the river. The dwarf birch is one of the least demanding pioneer plants and is found, bravely resisting any climate, along the extreme vegetation limits in the mountains and in the polar North.

10 Panorama from the Puija peak near Kuopio in the middle of the Finnish lake plain at 63° North latitude. As far as the eye can see there is water and forest, only occasionally broken by small clearings with agricultural settlements. In Finland the boreal coniferous forest extends to a North latitude of 72° thanks to the warming effect of the Gulf Stream.

11 The undemanding Aleppo pine is a valuable pioneer plant on ground denuded by forest fires or on karst slopes where water is scarce. Where young trees are grown in massive stands resin is gathered by tapping the stems. Even the numerous cones are strongly resinous and are used for adding a resin flavor to wine; this also acts as a preservative.

12 In Belgium 19 per cent of the area is wooded but only half of this is managed as fully-grown forest. The other half is middle or underwood, yielding scarcely any commercial timber. As an industrialized country Belgium therefore has to import over 140 million cubic feet of timber annually.

13 One of the most impressive oak forests in France is that of Bellême (Orne) which covers 6,180 acres. Oaks prefer deep soil; they need light and warmth, and they resist gales. They can grow to a height of 100 to 130 feet. Common oak *(Quercus robur)* and sessile or Durmast oak *(Quercus petraea)* cover 35 per cent of the forest area of France.

14 Rocky Mountains, Bow River Valley, Banff National Park (Alberta, Canada). In forest areas free from human interference the presence of a tree species depends on its vitality vis-à-vis its rivals. In damp locations near water, poplars *(Populus trichocarpa)* and aspen *(Populus tremuloides)* are the most vigorous. On marshy to dry soils stands of spruce *(Picea glauca* and *Picea mariana)* hold their own, with scattered firs *(Abies lasiocarpa)*. Dry rocky slopes are covered with pine *(Pinus contorta)*.

15–16 Intensive use of forests requires highways and trails. Over vast forest areas of eastern Europe and Russia, and in tropical areas, the forest railway has been the means for working and hauling timber. In thickly populated areas highways can so cut up a forest and damage its area structure that it can no longer discharge its functions. Both agriculture and the recreation facilities for the public demand adequately large forests. National and regional planning can ensure their protection.

17 The luxuriant rain forests in the equatorial estuary area of the Amazon contain an exceptional wealth of plants. The banana plants *(Musaceae)* with their leaves and stalks produce a stem between 13 and 16 feet high. *Musa paradisiaca* is native to South America; Africa has the plantain which can be cooked as a vegetable.

18 The National Parks in the U.S.A. contain numerous tropical palm species–the tallest grow to 165 feet–such as cabbage palmetto *(Sabal palmetto)* on the southern Atlantic coast, in Florida and South Carolina, and Cañon palm *(Washingtonia filifera)* in Southern California. Palms are exceedingly important as commercial trees; in addition to their better known products such as coconuts, dates, oil, sago, sugar, fat and juices, they also provide fronds for roofing, vegetable ivory and horsehair, and bast as well.

19 The Kurile larch *(Larix gmelini)* is native to the Kurile island group between Hokkaido and Kamchatka. The young shoots are bluish red and bloomed; the needles are rather stiff and curved like a sickle; the cones are dark red and 0.6 to 1 inch long. This fast growing tree with early shoots is regarded as frost resistant in Central Europe. The *Gramineae* species *Sasa* is related to the bamboo plant and comprises about 20 species in China and Japan. In contrast to other bamboos the Kurile species does not grow tall.

20 Tree roots absorb nutritive substances and water from the earth and anchor the stem in the soil, Leaf roots are developed by tropical trees on shallow soils and, like true aerial roots, absorb air.

21 The Virginian bald cypress *(Taxodium distichum)* is a summer-green conifer which sheds its short shoots every fall. The species name, *distichum,* indicates the arrangement of the needles in two rows. The flat far-ranging roots form curious excrescences in wet or swampy soil; these serve as respiratory organs. In its native North America the bald cypress often forms entire stands. The Mexican Montezuma cypress *(Taxodium mexicanum)* can reach a great age. Because it is winter resistant, *Taxodium distichum* is a favorite tree in parks.

22 The world's oldest trees are the bristlecone pines *(Pinus aristata)* in the White Mountains of California, where they form a forest belt up to an altitude of 11,500 feet but only reach a height of 33 feet. They are 4,000 to 5,000 years old.

23 Natural scenery in wood and stone: Bryce Canyon National Park, U.S.A. The Bryce Canyon National Park is situated north of the Grand Canyon and, like the many other National Parks in the U.S.A., presents nature in its original form, both created and evolved. But nature destroys itself: the twisted weathered tree and the pillars of sediment rock have been marked by the tooth of time. Amidst them, however, young conifers thrive. The rock has a striking yellow color which glows in daylight and phosphoresces in moonlight. The plateau averages 8,200 to 9,800 feet above sea level.

24 Grand Canyon National Park in Northern Arizona (U.S.A.), the world's greatest erosion area, cut by the Colorado River. The canyon is about 5,000 feet deep and it is possible to trace back the rock formations in geological history over 1,500,000,000 years. Moreover, this crowded space contains all the vegetation associations occurring from Mexico to Canada. The gorge is a barrier to wildlife: different species of squirrel live to the north and south of it.

25 Palm forest in Uruguay, South America. *Butia capitata,* called the Yatay palm in Uruguay, is used to cover extensive areas of otherwise treeless pampas. The palm grows exceedingly slowly and in 100 years barely exceeds a height of 20–26 feet. For a long time it was ruthlessly exploited: the tough fibres of its stem provided ropes and woven articles, its sweet sap was reduced to "palm honey", its leaves were used as fuel. Although these uses were prohibited or restricted by legislation, large portions of the palm forests have been destroyed. For the past few decades their survival has been threatened by cattle grazing. The animals crowd in the slight shade provided by the Yatay palms and young growth is nibbled off before it can develop. The unique forests can only be saved from total extinction by the exclusion of grazing livestock.

26 Yucatan, Mexico. The farming descendants of the Mayas obtain their arable soil by clear-cutting the primeval forest, usually after the few valuable trees have been removed by industrial enterprises. The brush on the cleared area is set on fire and burnt. Between the tall charred tree stumps maize and beans, the principal diet of the natives, are planted according to ancient traditional method. Small holes are drilled in the ground with a long stick and the seeds, carried by the natives in a gourd, are flung into the holes with a sure aim and trodden in with the foot.

27 Southern Sierra Madre, Mexico. To this day there are extensive unexplored primeval forests in the western and southern Sierra Madre, Mexico's largest continuous forest regions. Their exploitation, mainly by industrial firms, however, is progressing rapidly. In some areas well-planned highways are built with modern machines. As soon as the roads are completed the felling and stripping of valuable trees begins–especially the very numerous pine species. Clear-cutting is forbidden by law. The picture shows a mobile American skidder, equipped with rope hoist and power winch, at work in the forest. Haulage to the highway is not always accomplished with the desirable degree of consideration for the remaining trees.

28 Mount Rundle and Vermilion Lake in Alberta (Canada). A scarcely changed cultivated landscape with a storm approaching. The trees are cut in wide strips and the cleared area is not artificially reforested but covers itself with young trees grown from wind-borne seeds from the nearby forest.

29 Water lily lake in the Rocky Mountains National Park, Colorado, U.S.A. Water lilies thrive in calm water without currents. A mountain lake, untouched by man, surrounded by a thick spruce forest and steep mountain ridges, provides the best conditions. The highest mountain within the Park is Longs Peak, over 13,000 feet. This mountain landscape is a well-developed area between 10,000 and 13,000 feet above sea level and is visited by numerous tourists during the summer, from May to October.

30 Forest on the Kenai Peninsula (Alaska) destroyed by fire with subsequent flooding. Situated at 60° North latitude, south of Anchorage.

31 From the Atlantic seaboard, right across the vast territory of Canada all the way to the Pacific, 3,700 miles of highway link the west of the North American continent with the east, traversing a great variety of forest formations.

32 A troika, the traditional three-horse sleigh, in the Siberian forest.

33 The growth rate of trees along the forest limit is exceedingly low. The width of annual growth rings is measured in fractions of millimeters and it sometimes takes ten years or more for one growth ring to be followed by another.

34/35 In the inaccessible coniferous forests of Russia a great deal of timber is still transported by water. The forests are particulary vast in the Siberian taiga. Under Central European conditions this form of timber haulage would be too expensive and wasteful. European forests are extensively equipped with trails and cable-lifts. The last timber haulage by water in the Alps was on the Brandenberger Ache in the Tyrol on June 17, 1966.

36 Spruce woods of the same age after a snowfall. Being an artificial stock it was insufficiently thinned. The great density of the trees caused the branches to become stunted, allowing only slight growth.

37 Winter in a Finnish forest. The flexible branches support the heavy load of the snow. In the mountains and in northern latitudes the trees are slimmer to reduce the danger of fracture by snow.

38 In contrast to equal-age pure stands, in a selectively-cut forest the entire air space from the ground to the treetops is filled with needles and leaves (assimilation organs), ensuring a balanced forest climate.

39 Extraordinary root formations at Angkor, Cambodia, in the Chase Tree jungle. The West Cambodian jungle contains ruins of the Khmer empire (9th century A.D.) and these walls are overgrown with *Ficus* and *Bombax* trees. The roots embracing these ruins assume the strangest shapes.

40 The sequoias find optimum conditions between San Francisco in California and Vancouver. In 1965 three coastal redwoods *(Sequoia sempervirens)* were discovered in Redwood Creek Valley with heights ranging from 398 to 402 feet; they are believed to be the world's tallest trees.

41 Root system of beech: because of the shallow soil the roots have remained on the surface. *Fagus silvatica* is distributed in Europe from Northern Spain to the Balkans and from Italy to Denmark. *Fagus grandifolia* is distributed in the U.S.A. and Canada from Lake Michigan (Chicago) to Newfoundland. A hardwood of great commercial value for plywood, office furniture, parquet flooring, etc.

42 Bottle tree is the name given to trees with bottle-shaped fruit and also to those with exceptionally thick storage stems, as in the *Bombacceae* family. A typical bottle tree is *Chorisia ventricosa,* a characteristic species of the Brazilian Catinga and of the Gran Chaco thorn forest. The spongy timber, as light as cork, is used for building canoes and rafts.

43 The fruit of *Theobroma cacao* grows directly on the stem. The origin of the cocoa tree is in the Gulf of Mexico and in South America, where it thrives at an altitude of 1,000 feet. It was later planted in all tropical countries; constant temperatures of 75 to 82° F (24 to 28° C) are necessary for its growth. The cocoa tree bears fruit after four years; the fruit is picked twice yearly.

44 The elk's-horn fern *Platycerium* is not a parasite but an epiphyte, using the tree merely as its carrier. The water accumulated in its leaf funnel, together with mineral and organic substances, ensures its subsistence.

45 Strangler fig, a parasite, encircling an oak stem in the Everglades rain and swamp forest in the southerly tip of Florida (26° North latitude). The strangler fig is widespread also in the tropical jungle; it climbs into the tree crowns in search of light, gradually smothering and strangling them.

46 Lianas as climbers are rooted in the soil but develop their flowers and leaves in the topmost vegetation layer of the primeval forest. Only secondary internodal leaves develop in the shade of the trees. The creeper palm can reach a length of 1,000 feet.

47 Epiphytes are plants which live on other plants without obtaining their nourishment from them. In the North they occur as mosses and lichens, in the tropics there are a great many species which trap rainwater and humus.

48 Native liana bridge in the tropical forest of Guinea (equatorial Africa) at 10° North latitude. This "natural bridge" is entirely plaited from aerial roots and lianas and is suspended by strands of plants. The load-bearing cables are fastened to the branches of 230-feet-high trees on the banks.

49 Kauris *(Agathis australis)* in the New Zealand Waipoua Forest. Tane Mahuta or "God of the forest" is the Maori name for the impressive remnants of the former Kauri rain forest. These trees can grow to a height of 200 feet and reach a diameter of up to 20 feet. Their logs provide valuable timber.

50 Wind-swept treetops of the bush near Mile Bluff in New Zealand.

51 Native huts such as these are found in mountainous areas of the tropical rain forest. They are predominantly roofed with reeds and palm fronds.

52 The Japanese park-forests are harmoniously composed of the most varied tree species and are of great natural beauty. The care of trees is an ancient tradition in Japan and is

practised with particular devotion. The Japanese also possess the skill of controlling the growth of natural trees. They then reach heights of merely 12 to 20 inches and have the appearance of fully grown trees (dwarf trees).

53 The edible chestnut *(Castanea sativa)*, whose fruit is eaten, is a warmth-loving tree. Its natural northern boundary runs through Southern Switzerland, the South Tyrol and Carinthia. In Roman times it was deliberately introduced further north, along the middle and upper Rhine. The horse chestnut *(Aesculus hippocastanum)* belongs to a different botanical family even though the fruits of the two trees are similar.

54 The evergreen cypress *(Cupressus sempervirens)* is recognized by its dark green foliage, by its more or less square twigs and by its walnut-sized spherical or oval cones. Cypresses (scale conifers) were cultivated early in classical antiquity and are closely linked with human history. In modern translations of the bible the words "fir" and "pine" have been frequently replaced by "cypress". The hard and pleasantly perfumed wood of the evergreen cypress is exceedingly durable and was formerly used as building timber, especially for shipbuilding. The doors of St. Peter's Cathedral in Rome are of cypress wood; they date back to 1600 A.D.

55 Tree belts are capable of reducing wind velocity over a distance equalling 25 times their height. But solitary trees suffer deformation and stunting if continually exposed to gales.

56 In a number of countries, including Syria and in Yellowstone Park in the U.S.A., there are petrified trees which were alive 40 to 50 million years ago. Following the loss of sap the air spaces in the wood fill with mineral fluid and thus, over the course of thousands of years, become petrified. Silicified wood has also been found in the Saar.

57 Sunsets in the tropical forests near the equator have a high light intensity in spite of the almost horizontal angle of incidence.

58 The koala bear *(Phascolarctos cinereus)* feeds on eucalyptus leaves. Its soft fur is highly valued and, in spite of its amusing and gentle charm, it has been over-hunted. The authorities intervened only just in time to save it from total extinction, with the result that this typical Australian mammal is once more frequently seen in the east of the country.

59 The eucalyptus is the king of Australian trees. Of its 500 species the following are particularly well represented in Australia: *Eucalyptus camaldulensis* in Southern Australia, *Eucalyptus globulus* in Tasmania, *Eucalyptus regnans* in Victoria and north-eastern Tasmania.

60 The Amazon region is inhabited by hundreds of Indian tribes of different races, which speak in many different languages. They are of Mongoloid origin, of yellowish skin color and make a living by gathering food, hunting and fishing. East Brazilian tribes include the Bororo, Kariri and Botocudas, the Amazon Indians include the Tucano, Otomacos, Jivara and Tupis.

61 Bow Valley and Mount Ishbel in Alberta, Canada. Vast forest areas have not yet been economically opened up because they lack transportation facilities. Growth is very slow at these latitudes. Thanks to the vast forest areas of more than 740 million acres Canada possesses a highly developed timber industry. Forest covers 38 per cent of the country.

62 In the background an equal-age stand of spruce *(Picea abies)*, in front of it, in the clearing, a natural young growth of varying age, with a sprinkling of broadleaves. Soon the gap in the tall forest will again be closed by these young trees.

63 A magnificent common oak *(Quercus pedunculata)* in the Landes (south-western France). Its area of distribution, however, extends beyond Central Europe as far as Scotland, Leningrad and the Balkans. Its hard, durable wood is used for a variety of purposes, such as railroad crossties, bridge decking, shipbuilding timber, etc. A storm-resistant tree; it can reach an age of 700 years.

64 The transverse section of oak shows the wide early wood pores as a distinctive feature of the ring-porous wood. The late wood portion of the annual ring is radially marked by

the special grouping of contact and storage tissue. The radially oriented rays are in the photographed section only narrow. None of the up to 20 and more cells wide rays of oak is included. Magnification: 400:1. Microphotography: Institute for Microtechnological Wood Research of the Swiss Federal Institute of Technology Zürich.

65/66 Only with ring-porous wood, such as oak and conifers, is it easy to determine the age by the growth rings. With diffuse-porous hardwood, such as poplar, and semi-ring-porous wood such as cherry, the determination of age with the naked eye is difficult.

67/68 Ivy *(Hedera helix)* can use its aerial or gripping roots to climb up tree trunks or fissures in rock and walls to a height of 50 feet. Its evergreen leaves are 3 to 5-pointed when young and with increasing age turn oviform. In dense forests the ivy only grows up the side of those trees which has more daylight.

69/70, 73 The substances assimilated in leaves and needles are transferred from the bast to the remaining part of the tree. In this bast zone is also the cambium, the tissue which on its inner side forms wood cells and on its outer side bark cells. The outermost layer of the bark protects the tree against the weather. Bark structure and color are one way of distinguishing tree species. If the bark is injured the wood is exposed to attack by pests, especially fungi, and liable to destruction. Small injuries, however, can heal up, form scabs of bark callus and be sealed off.

71 The so-called fairy rings–the strange circular patterns of the fruiting bodies of fungi–are due to the radial growth of the mycelium below ground. Popular belief has associated them with magic.

72 The annual growth rings of conifers are the result of the differences in wood formation in spring and fall. The early wood has large pores and is lighter, while in late wood pores (the water conducting vessels) are smaller, the vessel walls are thicker and the wood therefore denser and darker. The age of a stem can thus be determined from a cross section, but two to five years have to be added to the innermost growth ring according to the height above the ground at which the tree has been cut.

74 The felling of primeval forest trees is accompanied by numerous dangers. In America, to avoid splintering through violent impact, steel ropes are fixed to the trees halfway up and their fall is thus accurately controlled. Thanks to this method serious accidents are nowadays rare.

75–77 The vast areas of the African jungle in the catchment area of the Congo are increasingly being opened up by mechanical means. Timber floating on this second biggest river of Africa, whose upper reaches terminate in the seven Stanley falls, is gaining in importance. In its middle reaches the river is between 4 and 5.7 miles wide. It is navigable along 830 miles of its lower reaches and has become extremely important as a waterway for timber transportation to the sea.

78 Elephants provide cheap and mobile labor in the tropical rain forest. They move the logs to rivers and canals or to roads for loading on trucks. Valuable timbers are shipped for export from Bangkok, the Thai capital.

79 Timber transport near Heinola, north-east of Lahti (Finland). The logs are cut in winter, dragged to the lakes and piled in bundles on the ice. In summer they are towed by motorboats to the timber-processing factories.

80 Timber transport on the Gâtineau River (Canada). From Lac Gâtineau the loose logs are taken south to the Hull paper mill near Ottawa, a distance of over 120 miles.

81 Timber floating on torrents requires a special installation, the timber channel, to protect the logs against splintering and prevent blockage and log jams. The picture shows the Heinola fall north-east of Lahti (Finland).

82 The Canadian primeval forest in British Columbia is worked by the clear-cutting method. At one time vast areas were cut down, with no thought of regeneration. During the period 1950 to 1960, lumber companies began to realize that, with future growth in mind, clear-cutting should be carried out only block by block to ensure regeneration from neighboring stands.

83 Lumbering in Western Canada (Port Alberni, Vancouver). The loading and transportation of felled and sectioned for-

est giants is done by unique methods developed from lumbering practice. Particularly massive trees are systematically left standing at certain distances and used to fasten drag and hoist cables. In this way the logs are hauled up over a large area and loaded onto trucks.

84 The length of the cutting edge is generally less with a one-man power-driven chain saw than with a two-man leaf saw. For that reason the roots of massive trees, which might later cause difficulty during transportation or in the sawmills, must first be split or severed before the felling cut is made with the power saw. Moreover, the direction of the fall is accurately pre-determined.

85 In chalky locations the spruce *(Picea abies)* is readily attacked by the heartrot fungus *(Trametes radiciperda)*. The mycelium of the fungus first grows in the bast of the root, kills the root cells, and then spreads through the above-ground wood, causing the wood to rot and turn a reddish-brown color. Spruce stems attacked by this fungus frequently show a bottle-shaped bulge at the foot of the stem. Another similar wood pest is the honey fungus *(Armillaria mellea)*.

86 The extensive forest areas of the North have not been fully opened up because transportation of the timber is uneconomical or impossible. Forest highways and forest railways are expensive whereas the power of the rivers is available free of charge. The trees are felled in the fall; in winter they are taken across snow and ice by horse or tractor-sleigh or truck to the frozen rivers and lakes so that, in May, when the thaw sets in, millions of logs drift down to the collecting pools of the numerous paper mills. The rafters, the cowboys of the forest, are strong and skilful men doing a hard and dangerous job.

87 Newfoundland is a Canadian island at 50° North latitude with ice-free harbors and ample precipitation (influence of the Gulf Stream). Two-fifths of Canada, or 38 per cent of its land surface, is covered by forest. Conifers account for 72 per cent of the total–fir *(Abies balsamea)*, spruce *(Picea glauca* and *Picea mariana)*, larch *(Larix laricina)*. Canada supplies almost 50 per cent of the world's requirements for newsprint. It is the second biggest exporter, after Sweden, of wood pulp and the second biggest producer, after the U.S.A. , of paper and cardboard. The world's largest pulp and paper mill is in Canada. Vast stockpiles of timber are kept there.

88 The production of charcoal in charcoal piles is based on the fact that with reduced air supply, wood does not burn but is charred. The heat is generated by gases from charred wood. The open-air piles have nowadays been replaced by charcoal ovens which produce tar and wood vinegar (pyroligneous acetic acid) simultaneously with charcoal. Wood is chemically composed of carbon, oxygen, hydrogen and nitrogen.

89 The bark of conifers was formerly used for tanning. Nowadays the substances needed for leather tanning are as a rule synthetically produced; tree bark is used only in the manufacture of particle board. Timber earmarked for cellulose and paper manufacture has to be stripped of its bark. This used to be done with draw-knives. Nowadays machines are being increasingly employed for this job, either in the forest itself or at log stores. The same applies to the stripping of large logs of commercial timber.

90 With simple tools, and with the experience gained by Indian tribes still leading a natural life, elaborately carved building planks are cut from banana stems. In this banana forest in the equatorial latitudes of Ecuador the trees reach dimensions not equalled on plantations where the plants decline after 20 to 30 years of harvesting and have to be replaced.

91 The inhabitants of the Brazilian jungle are skilled boat builders. Their vessels are of simple construction and are propelled by paddles. The picture shows a hollow tree canoe being shaped from a tree trunk.

92 The beach *(Fagus silvatica)* has alternate buds in two rows, producing the characteristic ramification of its branches.

93 The flowers of traveler's joy *(Clematis vitalba)* can be seen from July until September. With their four milk-white sepals and numerous stamens and carpels they form loose axillary panicles.

94 Of the many species of ferns about 30 grow in Central Europe, predominantly in the forest. One of the commonest forest ferns is the male fern *(Dryopteris filix-mas)*. Its fronds, whose stalks carry small brown leaves and are much shorter than the frond surface, are arranged in the shape of a funnel. Ferns can grow to an age of 10 years.

95/96 The ecological associations in the forest are most clearly seen in the plant communities on the forest floor. Their association depends not only on the nature of the soil, its water conditions and the state of its humus, but some of them actually form nutritional associations (symbiosis). With the aid of mycorrhiza (union of a root with thread fungi) many forest trees thrive more successfully in unfavorable locations.

97 The wood horsetail *(Equisetum silvaticum)* looks like a miniature tree and reminds us that in pre-historic times the horsetails were real trees. The plant occurs on moist or boggy soils, on waterlogged soil, and where the forest has been clear-cut.

98/99 Of the two classes of mosses and liverworts some forty species occur in Central Europe, mainly in the forest. The mosses are exceedingly important for the water storage of the forest since moss can hold 5 to 7 times its weight in water. The haircap moss *(Polytrichum commune)* is widespread throughout the world.

100/101 Lichen *(Cladonia sp.)* on a rotting tree stump in the Jura, north-western Switzerland. The morphological wealth of the plant world is particularly marked among algae, lichens, and fungi. Although trees and stones are often enlivened by the brilliant colors of lichens, these small plants and plant carpets with their minute forms, often visible only under the microscope, remain largely unnoticed and unknown. Nevertheless the lichens are widespread throughout the cold and temperate zones, and from sea level to mountain areas.

102 Club mosses are plants of shaggy appearance. Their stems carry projecting scale-shaped little leaves. The club mosses of pre-historic times were the *Lepidodendra* and *Sigillaria*. Most of our hard coal has been formed from

their deposited remains. Propagation of club mosses is by spores after a growth of 10 to 15 years.

103 Like the fern, the mosses show a pronounced generation cycle of alternating moss plant and stalked capsule. The capsule of the *Musci* opens by dropping its cover, revealing a circle of delicately structured hygroscopic teeth all round the capsule aperture. The mosses of the forest floor are valuable water reservoirs.

104 The inedible fruiting body of the stinkhorn *(Phallus impudicus)* resembles that of the morel *(Morchella)* but has a totally different development. The young fruiting body is a white oviform structure. At maturity the slimy hollow stalk pushes rapidly upwards, bursting the integument which is left at its base and raising its bell-shaped cap. This is covered with a greenish-black slimy fluid in which the numerous spores are embedded. A sugary fluid attracts insects by means of a penetrating smell of dead flesh. Flies settling on the cap of a stinkhorn are covered over with sticky spores and thus help to propagate the fungus.

105 Of the 470 fungus species occurring in Central European forests only about 20 are poisonous. The egg-yolk-colored chantarelle *(Cantarellus cibarius)* is one of the most tasty edible fungi. The false chantarelle *(Hygrophoropsis aurantiaca)*, which resembles it, has a more orange cap and a stalk that is brown towards its base. Other edible forest fungi are *Boletus, Lactarius,* the familiar mushroom, the honey fungus, and *Clavaria*.

106 Wild strawberries grow principally along the forest edge and in clearings. The very tasty berries are pseudo-fruits. They are produced by the receptacle's swelling after fertilization so that the real fruits (the small pips) are embedded on its surface.

107 The cowberry *(Vaccinium vitis-idaea)* is frequently associated with *Vaccinium myrtillus,* the bilberry or blueberry. Cowberry and bilberry are a sign of dry, acid crude-humus soils.

108 Sulfur-yellow polypore *(Polyporus sulphureus)*. The orange or reddish caps are piled on top of each other

in large clumps, with individual fruiting bodies reaching a diameter of 12–16 inches. They are found in summer on oak, cherry and pear, willow, etc. The thick soft flesh is edible in its young, succulent state.

109 *Russula rosacea* in oak and beech forests, frequently on acid soil. Red cap on pink stalk; flesh white and firm, tasting of cedar wood. Delicious to eat, but should be scalded and simmered before preparation. Not to be confused with *Russula rubra,* which is poisonous.

110 *Calocera viscosa,* a fungus suggestive of coral or a goat's beard. Fruiting body gristly, tough and elastic with a gelatinous skin. In prolonged dry weather hard and horny. Found on rotting conifer stumps, splintered wood and branches in summer and fall.

111 Fly agaric *(Amanita muscaria)* in birch forest or young coniferous forest at the young spherical stage; stalk and gills white; poisonous (muscaradine and myceto-atropine). Easily confused with Caesar's toadstool *(Amanita caesarea),* especially at the young spherical stage. Widespread throughout North and South America, Australia, Europe, and Siberia.

112 *Geastrum rufescens,* an earth-star, in coniferous and broadleaved forests. The young fruiting bodies are closed; on maturity they burst open in the shape of a star. Before bursting the integument is white; later it is pink and, in the flesh, shot with wine-red. The spore powder which issues from the spherical endoperidia is dark brown.

113 Tree seeds often germinate in the rotting wood of old tree stumps, growing up into new trees. The fleshy skin of the fruit of the mountain ash *(Sorbus aucuparia)* contains germination-impeding substances. The seed (pip) must therefore travel first through the stomach of a bird or animal before it can germinate. The berries of the mountain ash are sought out by the birds and were formerly used as bait by bird catchers.

114 A fire-watcher's tower in a forest destroyed by fire north of Prince Albert (Saskatchewan). Forest fires can never be wholly prevented in regions with extreme drought and frequently even form part of the natural life cycle. What seems a disaster to us is often a necessity of nature for the preservation of species. The fire is followed by the appearance of various pioneer generations of trees and shrubs and from them develops a highly organized forest association best suited to the local climate.

115 Forest clearance by fire near Polounaruwa in Ceylon (Sri Lanka). As a rule nowadays the forest is protected against fire in every possible way. Clearance is effected by clear-cutting with simultaneous utilization of the cut timber. Nevertheless many forests are still destroyed by fire, deliberately or accidentally. Settlers and road builders in the bush resort to this simple method.

116/117 Losses running into millions are caused every year by forest fires. In Europe half of them are due to careless human action, while in the U.S.A. nearly 90 per cent of all forest fires are caused by lightning. In the tropics the forest-destroying and soil-damaging technique of clearing forests by fire for a few years of agricultural use is still practised in some places.

118 The first National Park of the U.S.A., founded in 1872, Yellowstone has just celebrated its centenary. It contains a wealth of exceptional natural features, such as geysers, hot springs, extinct volcanoes and several canyons. Yellowstone Lake, at an altitude of 7,200 feet, is surrounded by mountains towering to about 10,000 feet. A particular favorite with visitors is the Old Faithful geyser which hurls its water to a height of 160 feet every 64.5 minutes. In addition to its gelogical features the park contains a great variety of wildlife such as bears, buffaloes, stags and moose.

119 Alaskan forest partially destroyed by a ground fire. Resistant species like larch *(Larix laricina)* have survived the heat thanks to their fire-retarding and insulating bark, and their tops have retained enough needles for assimilation. In contrast, stems protected only by thin bark have been charred.

120 Tree bark imprint in molten lava prior to its hardening into stone. Lava flows bursting into vegetation and inhabited regions cause total destruction of all living things–a natural catastrophe. Lava consists of various

liquefied rocks and therefore diplays uneven structures ranging from glass to slag-like consistency.

121 Mould of a tree trunk which was charred in red hot lava. The wood core has weathered while the exterior has been petrified.

122 In the south of France and in other Mediterranean countries pinewoods are still used for resin production. One pound of dry pinewood contains a third of an ounce of crude balsam. Its components are colophonium (70%), turpentine oil (20%), water and other substances (10%). The cluster pine *(Pinus pinaster)* is the principal source of resin. In the past the Central European pine, the Scotch pine *(Pinus silvestris)* was also tapped for resin but nowadays industrialized countries mostly manufacture synthetic resin.

123 The cork oak *(Quercus suber L.)* is a Mediterranean tree but spreads across Spain into Portugal. Its bark is 1½ to 2 inches thick and grows again after stripping. The stripping of the trees starts when they are 16 to 17 years old and can be repeated at intervals of 12 to 15 years. The most important cork oak forests are in Portugal and Spain, and these two countries also head the list of cork producers, followed by Morocco, Japan and Italy.

124–126 Every year millions are lost by forest fires, half of which, in Europe, can be traced back to human carelessness. In the U.S.A. almost 90 per cent of forest fires are caused by lightning. In the tropics in many places clearing by fire and (intermittent) hoeing are still practised which destroy forests and imperil the soil.

127 Plateau of Mesa Verde National Park, Colorado. The Mesa Verde National Park shows the effect of karst soil on vegetation. In the foreground an oasis with a little more water has come into existence but the mountain pines have already died of thirst and only the juniper bushes have survived. Slight precipitation at 10,000 feet altitude at a latitude of 35° (the same as Cyprus) and a cracked limestone subsoil, where the water seeps away, renders life possible only to vegetation on soil of steppe character, or semiarid desert. The much visited Mesa Verde National Park is subdivided by deeply carved

rocky canyons with cave dwellings over a thousand years old and ruins of walled buildings clinging to the steep rock faces. The ruins date back to Indians who had inhabited these parts for 700 years and then abandoned them–presumably because of repeated rainless seasons and a drought which prevented all growth.

128 The acacia belongs to the *Leguminosae.* These comprise 700 to 800 species, half of them confined to Australia. They are well represented in Africa, dominating in particular in the savannas, where they form thorny thickets or occur as individual trees, often with an umbrella-shaped top. The proper territory of the umbrella-like acacia is the open steppe where living conditions are tough. This is where the characteristic flat umbrella-top develops.

129 The zebra is regarded as a precursor of the horse. Its stripes can be pronounced, or less marked, or altogether absent. The true or mountain zebra *(Equus zebra)* lives in Central Africa. The African elephant is larger than the Indian. It inhabits the major forests of Central Africa and can be relied upon over difficult ground. Its diet consists of twigs, branches and grass. At liberty it is believed to reach an age of 150 years, in captivity no more than 50.

130 Some 500 species of beetles must be regarded as dangerous forest pests. The family of bark beetles, in particular, can become a threat to forests. The female of the bookprinter *(Ips typographus)* lays its eggs in the bast under the bark, and bores a tunnel for that purpose. From this the larvae tunnel out sidewards, producing the characteristic feeding tunnel patterns, resembling an opened book. Trees are particularly prone to attack by bark beetles when their sap pressure is reduced. That is why felled trunks must not be allowed to lie in the forest for more than a short time without being stripped of their bark. Whenever there is an undesirable increase in the bark beetle population so-called trap trees which have been attacked by the beetle, are felled and their bark burned or chemically poisoned. In this way both beetles and larvae are killed.

131 While the bark beetles block the sap circulation of the trees and thus cause them to die, the larvae of the long-

horned wood borers live within the wood itself and ruin it commercially by their tunnels. Pupation of the great oak or hero longhorn *(Cerambyx cerdo)* takes place in a massive tunnel. The generation cycle is three years, with the beetle hibernating in the pupation chamber. The tunnels become black as a result of fungi; that is why oak pest is also known as "big black worm".

132 Gale damage in a spruce monoculture near Berne (Switzerland). The nature of the damage differs from one instance to another. In the picture the stems have been snapped at half-height; frequently spruces with their flat dished roots are blown down whole.

133/134 In some regions of Switzerland and Austria, e.g. in the Tyrol, the forest line was formerly much higher and the forest belts on the mountain flanks were far more dense. Timber utilization, mountain farming and, above all, cattle grazing have largely forced the forest back. Where these forests once provided protection against avalanches extensive engineering works have now to be carried out to prevent avalanche disasters and landslide damage in the valleys.

135 Twisted growth is frequent especially with beech and pine. One differentiates between right and left-twisted stems, between heliotropism and anti-heliotropism. The cause is thought to be partly the rotating effect of the wind and partly hereditary factors.

136 More than 40 different spider species live in the forest. In a biologically undisturbed forest there are 5 to 14 spiders present per square foot of ground. The garden spider *(Aranea diadema)* belongs to the orb-web spiders; its webs can reach a diameter of up to 12 inches.

137 The leaf-cutters *(Attinae)* live in tropical South America; they are among the worst pests. In order to keep fungi in their nests they cut the leaves of entire plantations to shreds.

138 The jaguar species occurring in South America and Mexico *(Felix onca)* differs from all other animals of this family by its long tail; it resembles the leopard *(Panthera pardus)* and the tiger *(Panthera tigris)*.

139 The Canadian beaver *(Castor canadensis)* is one of the largest rodents, growing to a length of 47 inches. It lives in underground lodges whose entrances lie below water. In Europe and Russia, where another species *(Castor fiber)* used to be widespread, it was almost hunted to extinction for its precious fur and the beaver-musk it produces. Thanks to prudent protective measures the colonies have increased again, and attempts are also being made in Scandinavia and Germany to set up areas where the beaver is protected.

140 In addition to the black bear *(Ursus americanus)*, the brown bear *(Ursus arctos)* is also widespread in America; it even occurs in Europe. Its two subspecies are the Alaskan giant bear and the grisly. In the American National Parks the bears enjoy particular protection and have greatly multiplied. Bears have a predominantly vegetarian diet and only occasionally are sheep or other domestic animals attacked while grazing.

141 Reindeer *(Rangifer tarandus)* are a deer species living in herds. The domesticated animals in northern Scandinavia serve human uses as bearers of fur and providers of meat. The reindeer is the only deer species whose females also have antlers.

142 Male wapiti *(Cervus elaphus canadensis)*. In Europe the red deer *(Cervus elaphus)* represents the race. The English terminology for this species must be handled with caution. In America the term "elk" is used for the wapiti, and "moose" for the "elk". In England "elk" means the real elk. Further confusion is caused by the circumstance that there are elks with spatulate and others with tine antlers. The tines of the tine elk, however, are far less ramified and project horizontally from the head; the animal's neck is thicker and its shoulders are higher than the rear end of its body.

143–144 Among the 5,000 species, subspecies and varieties of the ant family the best known in the forest are the carpenter ant *(Camponotus ligniperdus)* and the red wood ant *(Formica rufa)*. The wood ant is of great value to the biocoenosis of the forest and therefore protected in most countries. An ant colony may contain more than 100,000 insects and dozens of queens. The temperature inside an ant heap is up to 18°F higher than the ambient temperature.

145/146 In tropical and sub-tropical regions plants and animals often have strikingly brilliant colors. The largest beetle in Europe is the male stag beetle *(Lucanus cervus)* which grows to a length of 2.4 inches. It lives predominantly in oak forests on the sap of the trees which it sucks from tree stumps or from injured areas of bark. The larvae take five years to develop in rotten wood followed by three months of pupation. In the spring of the sixth year the beetles leave their wood nest, in the fall they deposit their eggs, and thereafter die.

147 The moose *(Alces)* is found throughout Scandinavia, Russia and Canada, as well as New Zealand. Its characteristic set of antlers only develop spatules from the fifth year onwards. Moose feed on leaves, saplings and tree bark.

148 Doe and kid of the mule deer, big-eared deer or Venado Burro *(Odocoileus hemionus)*. Its habitat comprises the western mountain forests of Canada, the U.S.A. and the northern part of Mexico. In summer the animals keep to the high mountain ridges to escape the mosquitoes. The new velvet on the young antlers is vulnerable to insect puncture. Among broken rocks these deer move in a peculiar manner. In a trot they jump off simultaneously with all four legs and thus, with jerky leaps, they climb and descend the slopes. In size and color they correspond to the American white tail deer *(Odocoileus virginianus)* but the big-eared deer is heavier and distinguished by a black tail tip.

149 Most European snakes are not dangerous to man; even the adder *(Vipera berus)* only attacks if stepped upon. The snake's tongue serves it as an olfactory organ and it is shot out merely for orientation. Snakes lay eggs, but there are some, such as the smooth snake *(Coronella austriaca)*, which are viviparous.

150 All owls are protected. They are typical night birds and feed on small rodents and insects. The call of the tawny owl *(Strix aluco)* is a high-pitched "ke-wick", but its mating call in spring is an intermittent howl of "hoo-hoo-hoo".

151 The crossbill *(Loxia curvirostra)* in Europe inhabits mainly mountain forests and nests also in winter wherever the seeds of conifers provide food for it. It climbs like the parrots do, with the help of feet and bill.

152 The nest of the squirrel *(Sciurus vulgaris)* has a main entrance facing east and leading downwards and an escape hole at the rear. Its summer fur is rust-colored, its winter fur is greyish-brown; there are also black varieties.

153 The male and female flowers of conifers are separate. The erect female flowers of spruce *(Picea abies),* are brilliant red and already show the shape of a cone. After fertilization by the yellow pollen in spring they grow in length, turn downward and, when the seeds have ripened, drop as a whole. The cones of the white fir *(Abies alba)* remain upright and after maturity lose the scales and the seeds, leaving only spikes standing.

154 The woodcock *(Scolopax rusticola)* breeds in central and north-eastern Europe and winters in warmer southerly regions where, even in winter, the soil does not freeze. Its flexible bill serves as a drilling tool for foraging in moist soft soil.

155 The domicile of the cuckoo *(Cuculus canorus)* is Europe from the North Cape to the Mediterranean. It resembles the sparrow hawk and possesses climbing feet with opposing toes like a woodpecker: two toes face forward and two backward. As a brood parasite it has its eggs hatched by warblers, wagtails, redstarts, wrens, robins and other songbirds.

156 The jay *(Garrulus glandarius)* is domiciled throughout Europe and changes its location only in the northern countries during the cold season. It is one of the most gifted mocking birds and can imitate the call of the buzzard, the alarm call of a roebuck and even human voices. Its strident "raitch" warns birds of the presence of humans. The jay is a ruthless nest robber but also gathers supplies which it buries in the ground and in this way contributes to the spread of, for instance, oak and beech.

157 The family of woodpeckers and wrynecks is characterized by a long chisel bill and climbing feet; the tail, too,

is used as a support. The male of the great spotted wood-pecker *(Dendrocopos major)* differs from the female by its red patch at the back of its head. The horny books at the tip of its long tongue and its sticky saliva enable it to pull out bark beetles and their larvae from deep boreholes.

158 The cunning fox *(Vulpes vulpes)* is a well-known charac-ter in countless fables. In the forest it discharges the function of a health inspector by catching sick and weak-ened animals. For the past two decades, however, it has itself been endangered by rabies in Europe.

159 The raccoon *(Procyon lotor)* is a native of North Ameri-ca but has recently spread also in Central Europe where it is now a huntable animal. It frequently washes its food, especially fruit, before eating it. Raccoons are also farmed for their fur.

160 Like the fox, the badger *(Meles meles)* lives in the ground in a set which it digs itself. Unlike the fox, how-ever, its diet consists of snails, roots and the fruits of for-est and field. In winter it has a prolonged hibernation in its set and does not re-emerge until the first warming sun-shine in February.

161 The graceful roe deer *(Capreolus capreolus)* personifies the charm of forest wildlife. Delightful as it is to watch, it can cause damage in young forest plantations by nibbling young plants and rubbing its antlers on young trees.

162 Orchids are found mainly in shady mountain forests or on calcareous soils. The lady's slipper *(Cypripedium cal-ceolus)* is the most common species but it too, like all orchids, is protected. Its development from germination to flowering takes 15 years. During that time its roots feed on an underground fungus *(mycorrhiza)*.

163 The Turk's-cap lily *(Lilium martagon)* grows in forests. Its perianths are rolled back in the shape of a turban.

164 Traveler's joy *(Clematis vitalba)* is a liana which climbs up shrubs and trees towards the light. Its fertilized flow-ers, after the shedding of the leaves, produce hairy long-tailed fruits, thus enabling the seeds to be scattered by the wind in the fall.

165 Young growth of common maple *(Acer campestre)*. A small modest species of the maple family (which comprises over a hundred varieties) grows frequently as a shrub or small tree but is capable of attaining a height of 65 feet. The field or common maple is widespread from Scandinavia to the southern Mediterranean countries, in-cluding the western parts of Asia.

166 The tropical rain forests of South America, Central America and California are inhabited by numerous species of hummingbirds. The first hummingbird to be brought to Europe alive, in 1905, was a Gould's violet-ear *(Colibri coruscans)*. These minute birds, weighing no more than one-tenth to one-fifth of an ounce, are cap-able of covering thousands of miles in flight. When the bird hovers in front of a flower to suck its nectar its wings vibrate at a rate of about 100 beats per second. Be-cause of their magnificent metallic sheen they are also known as "flying jewels".

167/169 Passion flowers are among the most striking blooms in the plant kingdom. The stamens and ovary are sup-ported by a common stalk, known as the gynandrophore. The Italian botanist Ferrari saw in them the instruments of torture used on Christ; hence the name passion flower. There are about 400 species, mostly in tropical America; some of them produce edible fruit, such as *Passiflora edulis* and *Passiflora quadrangularis*. In Europe *Passiflora caerulea* is a popular ornamental and pot plant.

168 The vanilla also belongs to the orchid family. The species *Vanilla planifolia,* which is sold as a flavoring, is a native of Mexico and is cultivated in the tropics.

170 The Helicon banana is named after the Helicon moun-tain range north of the Gulf of Corinth, regarded by the ancient Greeks as the home of the Muses. The species be-longs to the *Musaceae* family. The species *Heliconia* in-cludes roughly 150 varieties. It is a native of tropical and sub-tropical South and Central America. In the West In-dies the young saplings are sometimes eaten as a vegeta-ble. The large leaves are used by the natives as a roofing material for their huts.